MOVING FORWARD

NEW DIRECTIONS IN TRANSPORT DESIGN

WITHDRAWN

HELEN EVENDEN

V&A CONTEMPORARY

First published by V&A
Publications, 2007

V&A Publications
Victoria and Albert Museum
South Kensington
London SW7 2RL

Distributed in North America
by Harry N. Abrams, Inc.,
New York

ISBN 978 1 85177 491 3
Library of Congress Control
Number 2006936582

10 9 8 7 6 5 4 3 2 1
2011 2010 2009 2008 2007

V&A Publications
Victoria and Albert Museum
South Kensington
London SW7 2RL
www.vam.ac.uk

Designed by
Graphic Thought Facility

Cover illustration:
NewStratos developed by
Christian Hrabalek, Serge
Porcher and Sergio Suchomel of
Fenomenon Ltd. See p. 23
Photograph: Anthony Bernier,
retouched by Fenomenon Ltd,
2005. © Fenomenon Ltd

Printed in China

MOVING FORWARD

ACKNOWLEDGEMENTS

The Research Development Fund at the Royal College of Art supported the research for this publication. Most appreciation is due to Clive Birch, Senior Past Master of the Carmen's Company and the Visiting Tutor in Vehicle Design at the RCA. Thanks are also due to Nina Berkowitz, Giles Chapman, Corinna Dean, Edwardo Galvis and his team, Caroline Hamiliton-Walker, Professor Dale Harrow, Jenny Jones, Stephen Jones, Joe Kerr, Merih Kunur, Sam Livingstone, Sam Luke, Libby Sellers, Mel Thomas, Wanda Polanski and Melanie Woods. For continuing encouragement and advice I thank series editor Jane Pavitt and her colleagues, especially Monica Woods. This book could not have been contemplated, much less completed, without the help and encouragement of Gerard. It is dedicated to our children Florence and Sydney.

AUTHOR BIOGRAPHY

Helen Evenden is a Tutor in the Departments of Vehicle Design and Critical and Historic Studies at the Royal College of Art where she is the Carman Research Fellow. She is also a faculty member of Boston University's London Programme. Her interest in transport design began as the Friends of the Victoria and Albert Museum scholar when she recorded the development of petrol station design and graduated with an MA from the Royal College of Art/Victoria and Albert Museum. She has curated a number of automotive exhibitions including **E-TYPE: STORY OF A BRITISH SPORTS CAR**, Flaminio Bertoni's **DESIGNS FOR CITROËN**, British cars for the **DESIGNING MODERN BRITAIN** exhibition, and a McLaren F1 Technology exhibit at the Design Museum. She has recently been working on curation for Beijing's new Automotive Museum.

6—13
GO —
DESIGNS ON
YOUR JOURNEY

IMPROVING OUR TRAVEL ENVIRONMENT IS PERHAPS THE MOST CHALLENGING AREA FOR CONTEMPORARY DESIGNERS.

Improving our travel environment is perhaps the most challenging area for contemporary designers. Vehicle designers, graphic and communication designers, interface designers, engineers and architects, textile and even fashion designers are changing the physical experience of the modern journey, realizing modes of transit and ways of organizing travel which our grandparents could only imagine.

Futurologist Ian Pearson sees the dramatic potential for technology further changing our journeys: 'We're heading into a world where you have dual appearances – physical appearance and your digital appearance …a lot of people will soon be using head-up display systems such as smart glasses, and mobile phone functionality will be encased in jewellery …you could be walking (or driving) into town with your navigation or tourist information coming through your phone.'[1]

Today we know that transport is a far more vital issue in everyday life than it was in the past, and our expectations for mobility are continually promoted by the transport providers. You only have to look at the colossal capital invested in shipping, rail, road and air transport, supported by advertising campaigns encouraging us all to travel more and more. Consumers will expect choice above all else, so they may select which mode of travel to use, and then they will expect that mode to deliver a moving experience rather than a bare transfer from A to B.

Yet, the greatest challenge facing designers of transportation is the environmental imperative. To girdle the earth, we have plundered and endangered it. The future of movement is in the hands of those designers who seek sustainable power, recycled materials and the freedom of all people to move when, where and how they wish. The wider world will expect responsible design, substance rather than style, cost-effective solutions, and socio-political enabling of ease of travel and transmission of goods.

In the twenty-first century, movement will be one key to relieving poverty and spreading prosperity, and its responsible development will arguably be the single most significant contribution to planetary stability. Modern movement depends on power and materials.

The history of transport is rich with amazing breakthroughs, when inventors and pioneers enabled new modes of transport through innovation in sources of power or vehicle form.

WE'RE HEADING INTO A WORLD WHERE YOU HAVE DUAL APPEARANCES – PHYSICAL APPEARANCE AND YOUR DIGITAL APPEARANCE.

IAN PEARSON

MODERN JOURNEYS
Five cities: Bombay, London, New York,
San Francisco, Tokyo
Photographs: Tapio Snellman and
Christian Grou of neutral.gs
2005

The key developments that modern designers have to move on from include Etienne Lenoir's self-propelled cart (1862), Karl Benz's three-wheel car (1885) and Gottfried Daimler's first four-wheel car with an internal combustion engine (1886). In the early twentieth century, American pioneer Henry Ford famously democratized access to the motor car.[2] International trade by sea has always been and remains the major mode of transit for the supply of goods, and the joys of travelling at sea still attract increasing numbers aboard cruise ships and (for the most wealthy) luxury yachts. While the romance of early train travel has been lost, significant amounts of money are still being invested to move more of us by rail above and below ground. In the air, the Wright brothers' first powered flight on 17 December 1903 signalled the possibility for the vast modern industry that is air transport.[3] Then of course we even made it to outer space: on 21 July 1969 Neil Armstrong became the first man from earth to set foot on the moon, watched by over half a billion people around the world.

Today we expect design to cater for more than function, and ideally all our journeys should be pleasurable. Above all, design for mobility is about moving people and goods in greater comfort and with greater efficiency than in the past. We must address the needs of our ageing populations with increasing longevity, new working patterns, socially mobile singletons, families in flux, the need and desire to eliminate exclusion through disability, and increasing regulatory and safety constraints. Most importantly the true cost of our personal mobility in environmental terms must be considered if future generations are going to be able to sustain the possibilities for global transport that we enjoy.

Our expectations for travel are high and yet we are increasingly aware of the environmental damage we cause by travelling. It seems highly likely that our grandchildren will look back on our generation as the decadent ones who wasted crucial natural resources fulfilling our insatiable desire for global travel and our consumption of imported goods. We have to ask whether is it really necessary to attend that business meeting in Sydney when a video conference in London is possible, or to eat that avocado in December. Greenpeace and other environmental campaigners recognize the need to re-educate us to change our behaviour so that we are less dependent on long-distance and petrol-powered travel.

PUBLIC TRANSPORT – SPORT EVENTS
PRIVATE TRANSPORT – SPORT EVENTS
Isocrone maps 45/90 min from
San Siro Stadium, Italy
Design: Systematica

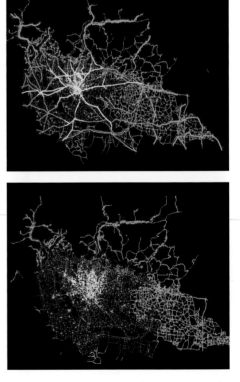

Mass transit is not only about people – it should also be about the efficient distribution of goods. The hypermarket and shopping mall are here to stay, altering our communities and how we move about within them, but the challenges of Internet delivery put further pressure on narrow streets built for domestic vehicles and not for lorries and vans. Automania prevails but is now restricted not by the design of vehicles but by congestion, which in many city centres has brought movement almost to a halt.

Professor Dale Harrow, Head of Vehicle Design at London's Royal College of Art, requires his students to address the needs for future mobility. Harrow feels that 'The opportunity to redefine private and public transport for the future is one of the most important design tasks of our time. It requires well-informed designers, able to create feasible solutions appropriate to time, location and most importantly to user need. In order to do this vehicle designers must be able to understand the needs of users other than themselves.'

H2O
Concept for an all-glass vehicle with visible new fuel-cell system, with water emissions
Design: Gareth Thomas
2004

THE OPPORTUNITY TO REDEFINE PRIVATE AND PUBLIC TRANSPORT FOR THE FUTURE IS ONE OF THE MOST IMPORTANT DESIGN TASKS OF OUR TIME.

DALE HARROW

Cities are also ageing and changing. In old cities infrastructures are creaking with wear – they are literally worn out by continual use. In most cities the conflict between our appetite for individual mobility and the collective responsibility we share for social and environmental needs remains acute. Many old cities are carrying out radical experiments to rebalance the relationship between the various modes of transport. Car, bus, bike, taxi and pedestrian are being reorganized into lanes or controlled by times of use. Today over sixty European cities are committed to the Car Free Cities Network launched in 1994 with a mission for 'developing, exchanging, and putting in place techniques and management methods for the reduction of the volume of traffic in cities …to achieve a healthier environment with improved air quality and sustainable urban mobility, to improve traffic safety, and to promote more energy-efficient mobility'. Private cars are therefore no longer necessarily the best way to get around our urban environments. Yet public transport still struggles to keep up with the convenience of the public car.

In cities experiencing development like the rapid transformation of China's reinvented metropolises and the development of the deserts in the United Arab Emirates into sky-high super cities, city planners have a new chance. The science of predicting traffic and pedestrian flows has become increasing useful for architects and city planners. Pioneers such as Britain's Space Syntax and Italy's SYSTEMATICA have developed techniques and advanced software tools to model movement for transportation, planning and traffic engineering. However, at present it looks as though the old models for the problematic relationship between the city and the car are being reapplied, just in different geographical contexts. Currently some of the worst traffic problems are in Dubai, where at peak times it can take more than two hours to cross the city.

H2R
Clean Energy Hydrogen Race Car
Design: BMW
2004

Throughout the twentieth century, visionary urban planners embraced the idea that the car would define the modern city. It could be said that the very idea of private transport for masses of individuals and mass transportation for all is central to the modernist ideal.[4] Modernist urban visions based on this ideal continue to affect the contemporary domain for transportation. Picture the futurist vision of modern urbanity: Sant Elia's multiple-layered complexes, Le Corbusier's schemes for massive metropolises with dense developments and straight-lined transit routes directly connecting them, and the more creative solutions of the early twentieth-century industrial designers, like Norman Bel Geddes's visions for 'Magic Motorways' with colour-coded lanes, and the Futurama pavilions at the New York's World Fair (1939), where people look like ants compared to the dominating presence of the cars produced by the corporations that sponsor them, notably Ford and General Motors.

Nowadays, we tend to accept the chaos and confusion of the contemporary city, while still expecting to find a range of transportation solutions suitable for all our needs. However, we are still failing to fulfil the potential for more pleasant and memorable journeys that the slower pace of previous centuries provided.

Only by examining the future of transport as a complex whole – from the expectations of the single car owner, to the global impact of mass travel on our environment – can we question what form transportation will take in the future. This book explores how this future is being shaped by design.

DRIVE – INTERFACE AND ENVIRONMENT AT THE WHEEL

TYPICALLY, THE VEHICLE DESIGNER IS SEEN AS THE STYLIST OF SLEEK AND DESIRABLE EXTERIOR SHAPES, ENGINEERED TO DRIVE SALES CURVES UPWARDS.

Typically, the vehicle designer is seen as the stylist of sleek and desirable exterior shapes, engineered to drive sales curves upwards. While design is still at its most competitive in the luxury sector, other, less aesthetic factors are also driving change. Design solutions are needed for cleaner, safer travel, eco-friendly power sources and materials, more secure environments for drivers, passengers and pedestrians, less waste and better opportunities for the recycling and reuse of parts. In terms of competitiveness, there is massive potential for product differentiation in both exterior and interior forms and details.

021C CONCEPT CAR
Design: Marc Newson for Ford Motor Company
Photograph: Ford Motor Company
1999

While working on the **012C** concept car for J. Mays at Ford, product designer Marc Newson explained that 'designing a car is like designing 500 products at once'. The potential for innovation in the design of each small element is exciting.

In order to foster such innovation, the car industry has developed methods of design practice that are unique to this industry. The increasing power and influence of designers within the motor industry is demonstrated by the fact that all the major brands now have dedicated advanced design studios, located close to their customers in world cities like London and Tokyo. Here the future experience of driving is being made real, a few years in advance of the models that we are currently able to buy and use on the road. As General Motor's Executive Director of European Design, Bryan Nesbitt, explains, 'It's Advanced Design's job to push on everyone else to get out of their comfort zones, to challenge conventional body styles, proportions, and methods of ingress and egress. They are the ones asking, "what happens next?"'[5]

Interior Motives, the motor industry's dedicated interiors magazine, observes that 'the car market is shrinking. Yet also expanding at the same time. There are less car companies and brands than ever, but the number of different models they make eclipses that of 50 years ago several times over.'[6]

YCC
Your Concept Car designed by women for modern people
Design: All-women design team at Volvo
2004

HONDA W.O.W
Dog-friendly concept car with
air-conditioned unit for pets
Design: Honda
2005

The relationship of many people with their car(s) is intense. Our vehicles are often the most expensive item we own after our homes. As Nick Talbot, Head of Transportation Design at Seymour Powell, points out, 'Your car is better designed than your house; the furniture is better designed than the stuff in your lounge, the car computer is more powerful than your PC.' Talbot continues 'cars are private bubbles; your relationship with your car starts before your drive it'. This statement is supported by the increasing expenditure on designer car showrooms and factories such as Zaha Hadid's BMW Plant, Norman Foster's work for McLaren, the Volkswagen Autostadt by Henn Architects with interiors and retail by Virgile and Stone, and Ron Arad's work for Maserati.

There is evidence that attitudes regarding gender, too, are changing. Traditionally one of the most masculine of design industries, some companies are acknowledging that both as consumers and designers, women may have a different perspective on appropriate contemporary design agendas. Although still in a minority, some female designers, such as General Motor's Anne Ascensio, are getting to the top of their profession.

It is clear, however, that the industry still has a long way to go. For example, Volvo may have a certain rugged masculinity in market perception, but 54 per cent of its American drivers are women. Its current design strategy, instigated by Peter Horbury and now under the direction of Steve Mattin, claims to have responded to this shift. The Swedish brand recently launched the **VCC**, promoted under the banner 'Your Concept Car designed by women for modern people'. The car's features, however, are indicative of a somewhat clichéd view of the female driver. They include practical places to put things, good parkability simplified by sensors and steering aids, limited instrumentation, low maintenance and high visibility, as well as an interior with adjustable heel-rest and coiffure-conscious headrests.

YOUR CAR
IS BETTER
DESIGNED THAN
YOUR HOUSE;
THE FURNITURE
IS BETTER
DESIGNED THAN
THE STUFF IN
YOUR LOUNGE,
THE CAR
COMPUTER IS
MORE POWERFUL
THAN YOUR PC.

NICK TALBOT

SKETCH OF DESIGN AND DASHBOARD CONCEPT
Ford Tough Luxury Truck
Design: Seymour Powell
2002

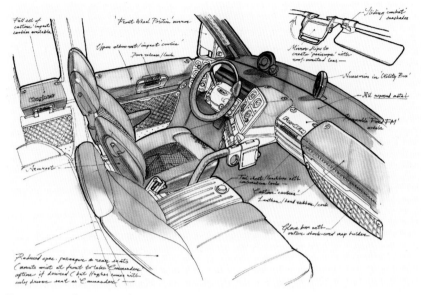

Despite such gimmickry, car interiors have traditionally been a neglected area, the second-rate cousin of the exterior design departments. Design critic Alice Rawsthorn regrets that 'The area of the car that designers always seem to forget is the interior. Automotive designers say that this is because traditionally they have tended to be judged on the exterior, so that is where they concentrate their time, energy and investment. But the interior is at least as important from the driver and passengers' perspective, because we spend much more time looking at it than the exterior. It would take so little for automotive designers to get car interiors right that I can't understand why they are invariably so wrong.'

Rawsthorn should be pleased with the increasing attention to detail in interiors. More and more car space is devoted to passenger rather than driver, and all the indications are that drivers may well become passengers in the age of systems technology. New design studios such as Gert Hildebrand's Design Department at **BMW MINI** in Munich are split 50/50 between exterior and interior. Hildebrand sees little division between the two teams, preferring collaboration rather than the rigid separation that was typical only a decade ago. This trend, coupled with our increasing dependency on technology, is generating change, but not all of it is positive. Giles Chapman, a leading commentator on the car industry warns that 'Inside, the dashboard, rather like the home, is being dominated by monitors, for satellite navigation, entertainment and a whole raft of other information that previously had to be computed in the driver's head. If it weren't for traffic congestion and speed-killing cameras, the drift of concentration away from the road and down to the TV screen would be killing off the driving population in ever-greater numbers ...'

INSIDE, THE DASHBOARD, RATHER LIKE THE HOME, IS BEING DOMINATED BY MONITORS, FOR SATELLITE NAVIGATION, ENTERTAINMENT AND A WHOLE RAFT OF OTHER INFORMATION THAT PREVIOUSLY HAD TO BE COMPUTED IN THE DRIVER'S HEAD

GILES CHAPMAN

DYNAMIC LUXURY

As is common among luxury brands of all types, history and heritage are powerful factors in marketing a product to a distinct and affluent clientele. Even so, contemporary design solutions are still employed by these heritage brands to maintain a relevant place in the market.

ROLLS-ROYCE PHANTOM
Luxury and status inside and out
Design: Sir Nicholas Grimshaw and Partners
© Rolls Royce Motor Cars Ltd
2005

Premier brand and doyen of British tradition **ROLLS-ROYCE** continues under new ownership. The new Phantom is a twenty-first century Rolls-Royce made in a state-of-the-art factory, designed by Sir Nicholas Grimshaw and Partners at Lord March's Goodwood Estate. Here Rolls-Royce has reinvented its core product without employing a past design, avoiding the retro trap, and offering its clientele a distinctive, luxury automobile.

Rolls also plans a sports cabriolet, and Burkhard Goeschel, a BMW director, talks of blueprints for 'a model that slots in below the Rolls-Royce Phantom'.[7] The Rolls-Royce 100EX, with aluminium spaceframe, presages the cabriolet, employing bleached teak decking, figured mahogany and dark leather to emphasize the aristocratic lineage in Ian Cameron's elegant design.

MAYBACH 57 S
Ultra-luxurious interior
Design: Maybach
2005

MAYBACH 57 S
Performance at the highest level
Design: Maybach
2005

Rolls has a pure German rival in the form of the **MERCEDES MAYBACH**. Founded by Wilhelm Maybach, known as 'the king of engineers' for his pioneering work with Daimler, Maybach established the firm bearing his own name in 1907, and his successes and engineering excellence were continued by his son Karl and now by the Mercedes company.[8]

Bentley, once the sister-marque of Rolls-Royce but now yet another German marque, invested heavily in a contemporary design strategy led by Dirk van Braeckel. Van Braeckel recognizes that 'From the very beginning, Bentleys have been quite reserved when it comes to design. It has always been recognized that Bentleys are much less ostentatious than rival cars of a similar price. The new Continental Flying Spur embodies that Bentley ethos of understated elegance.' The new cars embody Bentley's evolving modern image, retaining the understated but bold feel that its design team believes has carried Bentley forward throughout its history.[9]

CUSTOMIZATION

There is clearly a lot of potential for greater product differentiation and customer input into the specification of cars. Critics of the American car industry say the writing is on the wall because Detroit is still making cars the old-fashioned way. According to Cambridge University lecturer Mathias Holweg, 'The auto industry is still using the same techniques as it did to build the Model T Ford in 1908. …People want individual, customized products.' As many as 60 per cent of cars sold in Europe are built to order, compared to only 5 per cent in the United States.

Whatever the industry decides, individuals have always stamped their personas on their cars and will continue to do so. The need to personalize has become an extension of the automotive design process. Cars are often customized to reflect tastes, desires and individuality either by manufacturers who offer a wide variety of colours and specifications at the point of purchase, or later by owners. Since the Sixties, when the Bedford Dormovile and the VW Camper were redecorated in psychedelic glory, hot-rodders and truckies have made their own statements with go-fast mechanicals or customized paint jobs and lush or louche interiors, as epitomized by the Californian custom car. In Pakistan, Afghanistan, the Philippines, Indonesia and India, trucks with lavish designs proclaim economic, spiritual and cultural significance. In London a small fleet of distinctive and colourful **KARMA KABS** gives a Bollywood atmosphere to the insides of imported Ambassador cars.

KARMA KABS
Bollywood-style cabs
Design and driving:
Tobias Moss and Sasha Vitorovich
London
2007

RETRO FUTURISM

One trend that unites both the value of a brand's heritage, and the tendency towards personalization, is the recent popularity of relaunched models. The importance of brand, tradition and heritage remains central to much of the marketing and design strategies of many premier brands, and increasingly also to more accessible cars. Some reinventions are more conventional, representing resurrections of a past, long-lived form with updated materials, components and systems.

Developed initially as the 'people's wagon' of Nazi Germany, the pre-war Porsche-designed Volkswagen became the legendary post-war 'Beetle'. While at Volkswagen, the highly articulate designer J. Mays recognized the opportunity to remodel the Beetle for the contemporary market. 'The new Beetle', complete with vase on the dashboard, has proved popular. Mays in his later guise as Design Director of Ford's Premier Group went on to reinvent a number of other models, including the Ford Thunderbird and Mustang. He even coined the term 'retro-futurism' in an exhibition and book celebrating his design achievements. Mays has been extolled as one of five masters who are leading the world of design. Of car design, Mays says, 'At some point you've got to cut through the analytical logic and say "Hey, what's going to turn people on?"' Mays claims that he seeks 'classic timelessness' and sees the main challenge as 'making automobiles as relevant for the next century as they have been for the last century'.[10]

An interesting part of Mays's design strategy has been to employ non-automotive designers to experiment in car design. Marc Newson designed the 021C concept car with numerous innovations, like the pull-out drawer boot that could only have come from the mind of a product designer, albeit one with a love for things that move fast. Newson has since continued to reconsider what good-looking cars should be, and his **MNCELUX** concept car is another example of the retro-futurist approach to wrapping radical design in friendly and familiar forms. Supercar and retro-futurism combine in one startling design initiative, where the 1970s' iconic wedge-shaped Lancia Stratos with Ferrari engine has been resurrected. The **NEWSTRATOS** is a contemporary interpretation by the man with the world's largest collection of original Lancia Stratos cars. Chris Hrabalek of London-based Fenomenon felt that 'the car had to be instantly recognizable as a Stratos but it also had to use different design language in its forms, surfacing and details. It's not a retro car like the new Mini or VW Beetle.'

NEWSTRATOS
Design: Christian Hrabalek, Serge Porcher and Sergio Suchomel of Fenomenon Ltd
Photograph: Anthony Bernier, retouched by Fenomenon Ltd
2005
© Fenomenon Ltd

THE NEW MINI COOPER S AND MINI COOPER
Design: Gert Hildebrand at BMW Mini
2006

FUEL CELL
BMW has been researching the future
of mobility since the 1970s
Design: BMW AG
2001

The reinvention of Alec Issigonis's classic Mini was initially viewed with scepticism, especially in Britain. The original Mini was Britain's answer to the people's car and became one of the five bestselling UK cars of all time. In 2000 it re-emerged under BMW auspices in a design by Frank Stephenson, produced at Cowley, Oxford. That Mini has now sold out, with over a million units having been sold, and September 2006 saw the launch of the latest modification to the Mini – the R56 designed by Gert Hildebrand, which continues the traditions of the original Mini design DNA.

Hildebrand has presented a range of **MINI** concept cars and is also considering reinventing the Traveller. Mini has exhibited a hydrogen-powered Mini concept employing the **BMW GROUP'S CLEAN ENERGY SYSTEM**. This runs on liquid hydrogen produced from water using solar power, so there are no harmful emissions, depleting of resources or danger to the atmosphere. True to its legacy, the little car brought with it another design evolution – a hydrogen fuel tank reduced in size, which ensures that it only occupies the same space as a conventional fuel tank.

ADVANCED LIGHTWEIGHT COUPE
Design: Jaguar's Advanced Design Team
Photographs: Jackie Skelton at Exposure
Images, courtesy Jaguar World Monthly
2005

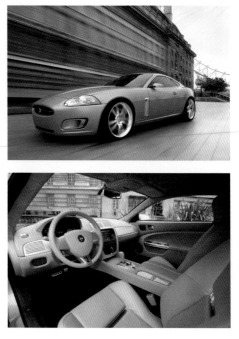

At Jaguar Design, Director Ian Callum has raised the design standards, returning the brand to the glory days of its founder, Sir William Lyons, who famously commissioned aerodynamicist Malcolm Sayer and engineer William Heynes to design the iconic Sixties' E-type.[11] Callum brought his experience of design at Aston Martin and assembled a team including Julian Thomson and Giles Taylor, who have 'demonstrated how well the Jaguar marque can achieve design evolution', observes Coventry School of Art and Design's David Browne.

XK
All-aluminium Jaguar
Design: Jaguar's Advanced Design Team
Photograph: Matt Skelton,
Jaguar World Monthly
2007

JAGUAR'S ADVANCED LIGHTWEIGHT COUPE is instantly recognizable as a car from that stable, employing a sensible design direction for a brand that relies on shape and posture for its enduring appeal – a design progress that marks out the quality car decade after decade. The ALC follows naturally from Jaguar's innovative work with aluminium bodywork, best demonstrated by the successes of the lightweight E-type. Lotus pioneered the material for volume production, while Jaguar as part of Ford's Premier Group developed the unibond method of aluminium construction, successfully applying it to the XJ8 model and the Aston Martin DB9. And, emerging in 2005, the all-aluminium **XK MODEL** has all the gadgets of a contemporary luxury car, controlled by simple touch-screen technology, set within the traditional walnut trim that Jaguar cabins are famed for.

CS&S (COMPACT SPORTS & SPECIALTY)
Powered by Toyota's advanced Hybrid
Synergy Drive system
Design: Toyota
2003

POWERFUL OPTIONS

Ever since carriage builders began to create car designs, styling has been the traditional means of product differentiation for the car industry. Now, increasingly, cars are also marketed on the basis of aerodynamics, safety, efficiency, maintenance and alternative fuel technologies.

'Travel is about using energy and moving people,' says David Nelson, Deputy Chairman of Foster and Partners, who has directed a number of transportation projects, including Canary Wharf and Expo Stations, bus shelters for JCDecaux and airports all over the world. Nelson reflects that 'Design for transport is one of the most significant design areas of this era – it has been for some time and will continue to be so. The dominant issue affecting future vehicle design is fuel.'

Petrol is a finite resource and the likely alternatives lie in fuel-cell technologies, petrol-electric hybrids, bio-fuel, ethanol or ethanol-petrol, liquid gas and hydrogen power. Dr Cedric Ashley, Director of EuroMotor, Birmingham University's research and development arm, predicts that 'the internal combustion engine will be with us for a very long time but the way fuel is made will change. ...Fuel cells will come when the cost of oil rises too far.'

CS&S (COMPACT SPORTS & SPECIALTY)
Seemingly a two-seater, removable rear canopies conceal a further two seats making it a true 2+2 sports car.
Design: Toyota
2003

CONCEPT-EZ MIEV
Mitsubishi's In-wheel motor Electric Vehicle
Advanced Prototype
Design: Mitsubishi Design Europe
2005

In car design, Toyota has led the way with its hybrid Prius and is continuing to experiment with concept cars like the **FINE-T**, which has electric motors in every wheel. A similar system also powers Mitsubishi's In-wheel motor Electric Vehicle **(MIEV)**, which has already given the Evo IX FQ-340 Lancer derivative a 4.3-second acceleration from 0 to 60 miles an hour.

Different manufacturers follow different strategies. **FIAT**'s advanced design policy favours the fuel cell, recognizing that it enables flat floor plans with drive-by-wire mechanicals, so that tomorrow's small car could be infinitely variable. After General Motor's President Rick Wagoner asked 'What if we were inventing the automobile today …what might we do differently?' the American giant looked ahead with its AUTOnomy project. Wayne Cherry, Design Vice President, explained that 'the base unit is designed for durability, not obsolescence', and that 'the car is designed around a fuel-cell system, with drive-by-wire controls housed in a 6-inch skateboard platform, so there's no engine to see over and drivers could move …to the front or further back', offering 'maximum freedom, maximum space'. That might well lead to customized bodies, maybe several for one customer, leased as needed.[12]

TRAVEL IS ABOUT USING ENERGY AND MOVING PEOPLE.
DAVID NELSON

FINE-T
Concept vehicle with in-wheel electric
motors and under-floor compact fuel-cell unit
Design: Toyota
2006
Courtesy Toyota (GB) plc

FIAT ECOBASIC
Module interior changes according
to the wishes of the driver
Design: Fiat
2000

Honda has launched the Civic Hybrid petrol-electric, and even the SUV market has acquired a hybrid with the Lexus RX400h. But Larry Burns, Research and Development Director of General Motors, believes that 'liquid hydrogen will be the fuel of the future …Hybrids are complex, expensive and heavy …Fuel cells are simpler than a conventional engine and a lot simpler than a hybrid …fewer moving parts, fewer wearing surfaces…' VW points another way with its Combined Combustion System, using synthetic fuel.

BMW, under the design auspices of Chris Bangle, will offer a production car with hydrogen-combustion engine as part of their 7 series. BMW's marketing material quotes Dr Manfred Stolpe, the German Minister of Transport: '…for sustainable mobility …hydrogen has a high potential'.[13] In Berlin, BMW have already opened the first public hydrogen filling station.

Now Daimler Chrysler is developing a plug-in electric hybrid and Mercedes has developed the **F600** Hygenius four-seat fuel-cell concept, utilizing the A-class platform. Daimler Chrysler are also applying sustainable power sources to public vehicles with thirty Citaro single-deck 'buses that store hydrogen and employ fuel cells located in the roof'.[14]

F600 HYGENIUS
Next-generation LED headlights,
a technology that will make its way
into production vehicles in the future
Design: Mercedes Car Group
2005

Of course, the idea of using alternative fuels, green gases and electricity is not new in transport design. As recent events prove, the instability of oil supply resulting in a fluctuating price will increasingly refocus designers on the task of prioritizing new technology applications for the use of existing alternative fuels. Already, Californians customize their hybrids with extra batteries, charged up at night from solar-powered domestic energy, and Asian owners fit a stealth button to switch on electric power up to a certain speed.

In different parts of the world, solutions are different. For example, in Brazil ethanol processed from sugar cane is used instead of diesel. In Umea, Sweden, buses using ethanol at a cost premium of 5 per cent have attracted more passengers and create less pollution.

F600 HYGENIUS
A high-tech compact car with a family-friendly design powered by a zero-emission fuel-cell drive
Design: Mercedes Car Group
2005

F600 HYGENIUS
Electric motors adjust the
Mercedes-Benz driving seat to the
contours of the occupant's body.
Design: Mercedes Car Group
2005

Oxonica, a nano-technology research lab linked to Oxford University, has developed a harmless diesel additive, one teaspoon of which improves fuel economy by 10 per cent and also cuts harmful exhaust emissions. Envirox comprises nano-scale particles that release cerium oxide, which lowers the temperature of the burning fuel, releasing more energy, reducing engine wear and producing fewer pollutants. British national bus operator Stagecoach is using it in its fleet of 7,000 vehicles and it is being trialled for petrol engines; cerium oxide is used in catalytic converters.[15]

Another intriguing development suggests that electric, hybrid or biomassive power should depend on place. The Stevens GVT (Global Village Transport) could be a car, van, pick-up, taxi, beach-buggy or ragtop, with diesel-electric hybrid town car, rechargeable electric open model or bio-diesel roughrider. The project is Professor Tony Stevens' brainchild.[16] With a polymer composite body, the GVT is inexpensive, simple to make and an intriguing response to Third World markets, which could attract the urban Westerner too.

SWAROVSKI CRYSTAL AEROSPACE
Inspired by the Trans-Australia Solar Car Race, Aerospace 'fuses nature with technology', each cell holding a single crystal to magnify the light
Developed in conjunction with Sharp Solar Europe, prototypers Coggiola, Swarovski Optical Laboratories and General Motors Europe Advanced Design Director Anthony Lo
Design: Ross Lovegrove
2006

IMAS
Inspiration for Honda's gas/electric
Integrated Motor Assist (IMA) system
concept car came from the bicycle
Design: Honda
2003

RAPID OBSOLESCENCE

At present, fuel economy is often presented as a 'lifestyle symbol' as much as speed and status are recognized as market drivers. For the ultimate racing cars and supercars, fuel efficiency and performance drive the design and styling. The lifespan of these cars is incredibly short considering the investment per car. Yet design for high-performance racing cars often sets standards that eventually trickle down to more accessible road cars.

Italy boasts more supercar makers than any other nation, with Ferrari, Lamborghini, Maserati and Bugatti all maintaining or resurrecting past glories, albeit under the wings of more prosaic brands. The nation also has some of the most established and influential design consultancies for the motor and transportation industries, including Pininfarina and Giugario.

The development of a **FORMULA ONE** car represents the pinnacle of automotive design as a rarefied process involving the most advanced materials and technologies. The design process for Formula One cars combines computer-aided design with computational fluid dynamic modelling techniques, simulation and stress analysis. The lifespan of the cars is short, with every car being redesigned each season according to Formula One racing specifications and safety legislation, as well as the demands of the drivers. Typically it takes six months to design, build and test each new car, compared to the seven-year development cycle for a standard road car.

SCRATCH
An Italian car that is enriched by scratches, revealing colours beneath the surface
Design: Uros Pavasovic, Royal College of Art
Vehicle Design
2006

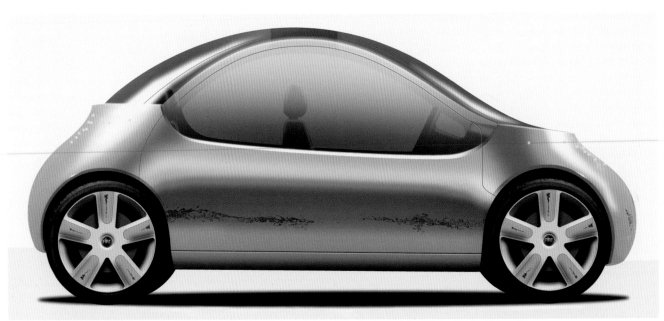

RENAULT F1 R25
Design: Renault F1 Team
Photograph: Luke Hayes

This field attracts many of the world's most talented automotive engineers and designers. For example, a design team of one hundred works at the McLaren Technology Centre, designed by Foster and Partners, at Woking in Surrey. Producing the 11,000 components of a McLaren Formula One car is a demanding process, requiring 4,000 drawings and accuracy to within a tenth of a millimetre. To optimize racing performance, the weight of each element, even the paint, must be minimized, and designers are constantly searching for more efficient materials and technologies to enable the drivers to control their cars at extraordinarily high speed, often in perilous conditions.

The **MCLAREN FORMULA ONE** designed by Gordon Murray and Peter Stevens is considered by many to be the ultimate road car, a vehicle hailed by the industry as a 'holistic design concept ...breathtaking in its clarity of purpose'.[17] The road-going Mercedes-Benz SLR McLaren produced in the laboratory-like facilities of the McLaren Technology Centre fuses gull-wing doors with a carbon-fibre composite body, a wedge with rearward cab, smooth underbody and six-channel diffuser with an adaptive spoiler that applies down force or acts as an airbrake. The speed of 208 miles an hour and 0 to 60 in 3.8 seconds makes this a supercar too.

WHAT IF WE WERE INVENTING THE AUTOMOBILE TODAY... WHAT MIGHT WE DO DIFFERENTLY?

RICK WAGONER

MCLAREN FORMULA ONE
Design: Gordon Murray and Peter Stevens
Photograph: Colin Curwood

SIZE MATTERS

Status and car design is a subjective issue. One of the key factors is size of vehicle; alongside brand and materials, this is the issue that determines the perceived importance and value of a car, in essence its status. Clearly many urban school-run parents are appreciating the advantages of the size and off-road capabilities of four-wheel drive vehicles, albeit at the expense of clogging busy streets and, despite low fuel economy, the increasing attraction for a tax-hungry Chancellor and increased fees to drive within a Congestion Charge Zone.

Giles Chapman observes that 'The modern sport utility vehicle (SUV) is the result of car makers trying to satisfy both male and female notions of "commanding", with their four-wheel drive and high-riding stance. Happily for car makers, impending legislation aimed at protecting pedestrians in collisions also calls for a relatively high – albeit protrusion-free – frontal area. So cars have become visually bulkier, less svelte, and need to employ ever-more adventurous surface design tricks to layer on "character".'[18]

The genre originally developed from four-wheel drive off-roaders, which were in turn inspired by the Second World War jeep, a Bantam-Willys hybrid that was simply designed and engineered. The CJ-2A, marketed with the slogan 'born for war – ready for peace', morphed into the Wrangler Jeep. Now this ubiquitous typology has reverted to type, with the Humvee hybridization of the US Army's **HUMMER** troop carrier, itself an apparently endangered military species. New Hummers with sound systems as large as the vehicles themselves are popular vehicles of choice for the Bling generation.

THE MODERN SPORT UTILITY VEHICLE (SUV) IS THE RESULT OF CAR MAKERS TRYING TO SATISFY BOTH MALE AND FEMALE NOTIONS OF 'COMMANDING', WITH THEIR FOUR-WHEEL DRIVE AND HIGH-RIDING STANCE.

GILES CHAPMAN

Land Rover's Range Stormer sports tourer reflects the classic brand's image, giving its bonnet, roofline, overhang and waistline a new sharpness and visual strength. Its interior is simple, clean and intimate, equipped with a fuel gauge without the needle, just a lowering liquid level.

Ford's **SYNUS** concept car, a Detroit experiment towards a small American car in a country dominated by large cars and pick-ups, has an almost van-like profile. It picks up the machismo image with a brutal front, chunky bumpers and doors like bank vaults, with dial combination locks and vault style spinners. Inside, the SYNus deploys simple, rounded lozenge forms, glowing orange light beads, reversible front seats, soft padded memory material and a giant LCD screen inside the rear door. Like a club 'chill-out' room, it suggests pleasure at leisure. In contrast, perhaps Ford's **MODEL U** made from recycled and sustainable materials is an experiment pointing towards the possibility of a greener SUV.

MINI COAT
Upgradeable fashion for iconic cars
Design: Serge Porcher
Fashion4cars.com
2004

HUMMER OR HUMDINGER
For the people with everything –
the mini Hummer golfbuggy
Photograph: Gerard Evenden
2006

AMBIENCE

Other ventures in vehicle design have attempted to merge cars more closely with the fashion and lifestyle industries. Such attempts employ the ambient tricks of lighting and in-car entertainment systems to achieve this.

The designer Terence Conran, better known for furniture and restaurants, has collaborated with David Godber of Nissan's London studio to refine the **NISSAN CUBE**. Conran has applied Japan's nationally characteristic 'Wa' calming influence in his design language, using the circle and pure straight lines to define and soften the new Cube. The pepper-pot rectilinear radiator grille houses circular lighting in front; behind, a vertically hinged door spans the vehicle. Bright red headrests like cough lozenges say 'stop and see'. The wheels are concentrically rippled, and interior vents, gear-stick and grilles are all circular. The result: an upright, perky box for today, containing many design cues for the future.

Light has always been an important factor in car design. Today the analysis of natural and artificial light is becoming increasingly important to car design, both for interior ambience and exterior profile. Hyundai's E3 concept uses a tinted glass roof with a floating opaque panel that carries courtesy lights to generate a simpler version of the friendly cabin. Mazda is among those including LED headlamps, in this case with the Ibuki (or 'breathing new energy into') concept forerunner of a new MX-5, with its ID card, keyless entry, and combined audio speaker/air ducts.

NISSAN CUBE
The original Cube and the later three-row Cube Cubic explore the latent use of materials
Design: Conran + Partners collaboration with Nissan
2003

Existing lighting now uses plastic lenses, xenon gas instead of filament, and may soon feature 'bent' light, which leads the car round the bend. Light emitting diodes (LEDs) are emerging, using less energy, outlasting current lamps and, due to their compactness, permitting entirely new configurations, not only for the lamps, but also for their positioning and therefore the shape of the car. Nissan's Actic concept car with roof video projection boasts a host of features, including a key fob which holds passenger preferences, settings for audio and climate control, email and navigation aids, and a portable hard drive.

Mark Lloyd's Citroën C-Airlounge and the **C-AIRPLAY** concept point the way for future people carriers, with expanses of glass and sensitive uses of lighting creating a soft and comfortable environment. At last light plays a part in 'furnishing' the car and the atmosphere within it. With emergent light-bearing materials, this approach marks the beginning of a trend towards 'living rooms on wheels'.

Citroën innovated for decades with distinctive, futuristic design and advanced engineering, especially in suspension. We all adored the quirky, immensely practical and long-lasting Deux Chevaux (2CV) and the architect's favourite is often the DS, or goddess, both by Italian-born Flaminio Bertoni. Now, a young Frenchman, Gilles Vidal, Head of Advanced Design at Citroën, talks about the 'magic, art and technology' employed by the brand. In the new century it is the detail rather than the grand design statements that distinguishes them. The diesel hybrid Citroën C4, with its unusual steering wheel, is typical: the hub housing the principal switches remains still when the wheel is turned, but little in the car's exterior signals the changes present in the innovative vehicle, such as the lane-departure warning-system device aimed at helping tired drivers.

MODEL U
An environmentally responsible SUV (sports utility vehicle), with hemp seating and various recycled materials.
Design: Ford Motor Company Ltd
2004

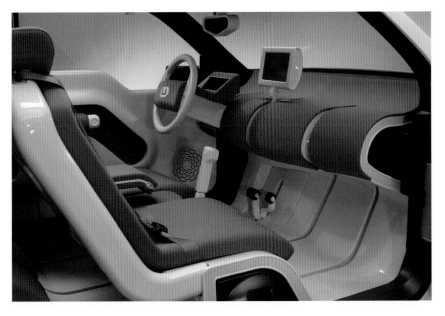

FORD SYNUS
More military vehicle than runabout
around-town; a gigantic LCD screen fills
the interior side of the tailgate
Design: Ford Motor Company Ltd
2005

ON THE ROAD

Since guided strips embedded in tarmac were first considered a possibility, now the pace of research and development in telematics predicates a substantive shift in the way we use cars and the way they respond to us.

Telematics is a diverse field that includes satellite navigation, remote diagnostics and repair, and the ability for cars to drive themselves. Honda's Lane Keeping Assist System, featuring in the 2006 Accord Executive automatic, employs camera-sourced lane recognition linked to vehicle control and 'intelligent' cruise control, which uses radar in the front grille to maintain distance between vehicles (something that Jaguar developed in 1999 and called adaptive cruise control). Wander five centimetres off course, and steering torque increases to the point where the driver has to correct.

Sophisticated sensor systems already result in cars being able to recognize their drivers. Frank M. Rinderknecht's Rinspeed Senso senses the driver biometrically, using fingerprint recognition to store personal data for different drivers and 'set' the car appropriately. The aim is for the car to establish the driver's state of mind, by measuring the pulse and recording driving behaviour it sets its own ambience: projecting appropriate smell, sound, light and colour in order to generate a positive mental attitude or 'relaxed attentiveness', akin to Zen. Crime is covered, too – by using GSM technology the system phones for help if the car is attacked.

The RAC Foundation foresees an electronic licence, without which the car will not start. Another proposal envisages an electronic vehicle licence that empowers the driver according to qualification – grading driver skills and categorizing vehicle types. Such a licence would record accidents and convictions, insurance and route access, and possibly even parking.

Technology is not confined to cars, as seat-belt detection cameras (used in Holland and Israel), white-line crossing road sensors (Italy), roadside breath-testing equipment (UK), event data recorders (trialling in the UK), and mobile data terminals for police and police car number plate recognition devices monitor drivers. In-car black boxes (UK) and 'alcolocks' (Sweden) are trialling, to monitor and correct driver behaviour. Security chips that will be satellite-readable and provide unique vehicle identity, eliminating escape from speed cameras and immobilizing stolen cars, are being investigated by the European Union.[19]

Developments are also evident on the road. Astucia is pioneering its intelligent solar-powered cat's eyes. Already in use in Holland, France and Italy, they light up in a range of colours, reflecting road conditions – blue for ice, red for other hazards – and can incorporate speed cameras.

I BECAME THE FIRST ARCHITECT TO HAVE A MEDIA LABORATORY OF MY OWN WITHIN MY STUDIO, A PLACE WHERE CREATIVE PEOPLE WITH MANY DIFFERENT TALENTS MET AND WORKED TOGETHER... OUR MAIN FOCUS WAS THE BORDER BETWEEN ARCHITECTURE AND THE ELECTRONIC MEDIA.

CHRISTIAN MOELLER

ULTRA
An electric vehicle system employing
automatic guidance along an ULTra personal
rapid transit (PRT) 1 km test track in Cardiff
Design: Advanced Transport Systems Ltd
2002

INFO-MOTION
Adapting the car cockpit to future needs
Design: Serge Porcher, Helen Hamlyn
Research Centre, Royal College of Art
Research Partner: Visteon
2005

SIT BACK AND RELAX

The interior driving environment is improving all the time, but traffic is increasing, causing congestion and other issues that reduce the pleasure of car travel for both driver and passenger. As our lives become more complex, drivers will be given more aids and more choice. Many of the innovations described so far indicate that advance research is often targeted at the high-end, status-car owner. However, new technology may also facilitate car-sharing schemes, many of which already exist in Europe and the United States. In the future more people may well choose to hire, not own, vehicles, particularly in the city environment, and, as the built environment changes, they will almost certainly choose driverless options as they emerge.

RIDE – TWO-WHEELERS

THE BICYCLE PREPARED THE WORLD FOR THE MOTOR CAR, FOR IT BROUGHT INDIVIDUAL MOBILITY TO EVERYONE.

ASYMETRIC BIKE
Concept for new frame
Design: Nick Rawcliffe
2005

TRICON
Concept for hire-bikes with no exposed
working parts
Design: Tom Eaton
2004

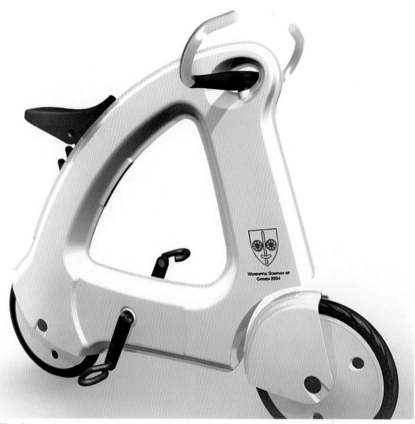

The bicycle prepared the world for the motor car, for it brought individual mobility to everyone. Cycling remains perhaps the most healthy and independent way to travel, since a cyclist is both driver and passenger. However, due to the interface of bike, motorbike and car in the limited space of city streets, urban cyclists face the immediate dangers of vehicular traffic and the longer term risks of breathing in pollutants, not to mention the problems of out-of-use storage such as theft and vandalism.

Now, as the motor car begets problems of congestion, pollution, and – with the inexorable rise in oil prices – cost, more and more people are once again taking a second look at two-wheeled options.

Public cycle systems in European cities where people hire bikes for nominal cost demonstrate that the bicycle can still serve effectively as a valuable mode of individual mass transport. Bike sharing may work in cities like Copenhagen, Lyon and Amsterdam, where bikes are sponsored or subsidised by government, but the concept has yet to achieve global coverage. In Copenhagen 2,500 'free' bikes each cost 20 kroner to release from their racks, refundable on return. Visitors have noted the poor state of the bikes and often prefer taxis or the city's efficient zoned bus/train service, with its clockwork precision and multiple tickets available everywhere, like the system in Budapest's tram-bus-trolley-metro-suburban rail infrastructure, where crossover tickets can be bought in bulk.

BAMBOO MTB BIKE
Design: Brano Meres, Slovakia, BME
www.bmeres.com
2004

MN02 BICYCLE BIOMEGA
Design: Marc Newson
Photograph: Tue Schiorring

Cyclist Tom Eaton's **TRICON** design addresses the challenge for durable bikes that could be available via sponsorship or club membership to subscribers in a given vicinity. Eaton has reinvented the bicycle's form, which is made from woven plastic, as light, smooth-surfaced and vandal-resistant, and by enclosing all moving parts there is no possibility of oil-chain marks. Capable of cost-efficient mass production, Tricon points the way for private and public cycle design. A similar enclosed design by Nick Rawcliffe with some elegant detailing is at the prototype stage.

The eco-friendly Californian **CALFEE** bamboo bike reflects a major manufacturer's exploration of organic materials. Following the 1980s' developments by Cannondale and Trek of aluminium frames, space-age carbon fibre and titanium innovations, and traditional steel with higher strength alloys and smaller diameter tubes, Calfee has used bamboo as an alternative to carbon fibre. This is a 1900s' idea with 2005 adhesive technology. So far production has been limited to 100 cult customers, for material of the right dimensions and quality is hard to find, but the project demonstrates the industry's response to societal pressure for environmentally suitable materials in manufacture.

Marc Newson developed the materials' component even further in his design for Denmark's **BIOMEGA**, which aims to persuade Danes to swap cars for bikes. He employed aviation's new super-forming technology to construct a weld-free aluminium frame, with the cables stored inside the tube, the headset connected to the seat, and then the rear wheel and all surplus detail eradicated.

IT WAS IMPORTANT... TO DEMONSTRATE THAT NEW TECHNOLOGIES DON'T HAVE TO BE WRAPPED UP IN A DULL PRODUCT'
NICK TALBOT

ECO-ENERGY-POWERED BIKES

Some say urban mobility is best served by powered two-wheelers that use less fuel and occupy less space in dense cities, so motorcycles are an important if more dangerous option.

Concern for the environment underpins Seymour Powell's fuel-cell technology motorbike for Intelligent Energy. The bike's loving design studio, headed by Richard Seymour and Dick Powell, with transportation design directed by Nick Talbot, seized the opportunity to design an eco-bike that met the design criteria of the bike enthusiasts. Talbot enthuses that the well-received bike 'is light, fast and fun, usable, useful and great-looking', adding that 'it was important …to demonstrate that new technologies don't have to be wrapped up in a dull product'.

The **ENV** (emissions neutral vehicle) two-wheeler uses the Intelligent Energy Core – multi-layered, thin metal sheets as membrane electrode assemblies encased in aluminium, part-covered in a micro-etched, textured and durable shell – for heat dissipation and visual effect. The core is detachable, and delivers 1 kilowatt, enabling up to 50 miles an hour for four hours and a hundred miles.

The bike is gearless, has high clearance and is acutely responsive, with an aluminium frame and batteries that can deliver 6 kilowatts under acceleration. Fuel cells and batteries together produce 8 horsepower, yet the bike is almost silent. Talbot designed the core as 'a stand-alone project, giving this radical fuel cell its due as a beautiful, valuable and useful energy resource'.

Executive of the Intelligent Energy company Harry Bradbury accepts that 'There's been a certain amount of scepticism over the future of a hydrogen infrastructure and economy', but the 'future might be coming a bit sooner than you think'.

CORE
ENV bike
Design: Seymour Powell
2006

ENV BIKE
Design: Seymour Powell
2006

Designer Peter Naumann has taken the three-wheeler into a new dimension with his **CLEVER** design for a Compact Low Emission Vehicle for urban transport. The project was developed under the initiative of the Technical University of Berlin with EU Commission funding and is now supported by BMW. The concept is indeed clever: as a city vehicle for two people it requires very little space, weighs very little, and has very low consumption and therefore also very low emissions. Bike engine noise may be an irritant to most (although it is loved by riders), but the silencing of engines poses other safety issues. Since future fuel-cell technology may well mean more silent vehicles, including buses, Porsche sees a need to compensate by playing alternative noises, if only for reasons of pedestrian safety. The idea is not new and will be recognized by children listening for ice-cream vans.

Yamaha's Dolsa Wind is an electric scooter that is virtually silent. The project's objective is aimed to create a pleasant zone of sound around the driver, so that he can hear the wind passing over the wheels. However, it is clearly not about improving safety, as its silence may make it a menace to pedestrians.

CLEVER (COMPACT LOW EMISSION VEHICLE FOR URBAN TRANSPORT)
Lightweight city vehicle for two people
Initiative of the Technical University of Berlin, Institute for Motor Vehicles, with support from the 5th Framework Programme of the EU Commission
Supported by BMW
Design: Peter Naumann, naumann-design
2006

REST –
THE PASSENGER EXPERIENCE

PASSENGER JOURNEYS IN CARS, ON BUSES AND COACHES, ABOARD TUBES AND TRAINS, IN AEROPLANES AND ON BOATS, SHOULD BE ENJOYABLE EXPERIENCES, RATHER THAN ORDEALS.

Passenger journeys in cars, on buses and coaches, aboard subways and trains, in aeroplanes and on boats, should be enjoyable experiences, rather than ordeals. Issues of maintenance and durability may necessitate a more utilitarian design approach to that of the private car, but if anything the design challenge is greater and more complex.

Designer and founder of OMK Rodney Kinsman suggests that, 'One should not distinguish between modes of transport. For mass transportation people expect the same standards. Now travel is travel. It is consistent. Passengers do not equate travel by sea, rail or air as different. They have the same expectations.'

Due to advances in ergonomics, materials, lighting and communications, passengers need no longer be trapped in a static environment. Journey time can now be part of the working day. Commuters can talk on the phone, send emails and be highly productive on their way to work or foreign appointments. The negative side of such advances obviously includes annoyance to fellow passengers, so designers are increasingly generating techniques to zone areas for privacy and concentration.

Perhaps our most memorable journeys are for pleasure. Many critics lament the lost romance of air, sea and train travel, although access to such privileges was restricted to the affluent few.

The United Nations predicts that urban populations will increase by 27 per cent by 2030 – a recipe demanding more and better mass transit, yet the car continues to sell in ever-increasing numbers.[20] The challenge for designers today is therefore to improve the environment of mass transit, using economies of scale to provide the quality of design that will benefit us all.

In London Bread and Circuses, critic Jonathan Glancey argues that the quality of public services, particularly transport, determines the quality of a city.[21] Acting as levellers across class, race and social divisions, they must number among the truly democratic public spaces. The image or design of a city's transport facilities, both vehicles and infrastructure, determine to a high degree our perception of the place. One only has to look at a postcard of London to see that the identity of the city is embodied in its buses, Tube and taxis.

NOW TRAVEL IS TRAVEL. IT IS CONSISTENT. PASSENGERS DO NOT EQUATE TRAVEL BY SEA, RAIL OR AIR AS DIFFERENT. THEY HAVE THE SAME EXPECTATIONS.
RODNEY KINSMAN

LONDON TRANSPORT

The London bus originally came from France, and London's bus system was a French 'steal' too. George Shillibeer's nineteenth-century concept offered the public a collective horse-drawn transit system that included a library in every vehicle. Unsurprisingly, Shillibeer went bust in 1832.

Transport design played its part with the Great Exhibition of 1851, when business peaked, canny operators combined in cartels, and French entrepreneurs bought into the London cartels, formed the LGOC and laid the ground for London Transport.

Many of the most famous examples of London Transport design were commissioned by Frank Pick, a Lincolnshire-born solicitor who joined the Underground Group in 1906 and regularly travelled the length and breadth of the network, often late at night, to check that every detail was up to scratch.[22] Convinced that London Transport should be an exemplar of design excellence, Pick commissioned work of the highest quality for everything from station architecture, to moquette seat fabrics and artists' posters.

In design terms London Transport's corporate imagery peaked with the iconic Underground map, designed by electrical engineer Harry Beck and incorporating Edward Johnson's sans serif typeface and roundel. Today Transport for London (TfL) continues to engage with its heritage at London's Transport Museum, reopened in 2007 with its new Futures Gallery, highlighting transport design year on year.

The unique and impressive design heritage of the organization encouraged Saskia Boersma and David Ellis of TfL to recruit designers like Ella Roran and Natasha Marshall to extrapolate from London Transport's past designs. Selecting the best of work by the likes of Frank Pick and Hans Unger, the contemporary designers created new products that were showcased in a customized Routemaster at the Milan Furniture Fair. Underground map picnic rugs, 1970s' Tube and bus-seat pattern sheets and bags, Routemaster Rocks coasters, a strap-hanger hat stand and kitchen fabrics are among the progressive products, taking transport design into Heal's, the Conran Shop and the Printemps store in Paris, among many selective outlets. Clearly, contemporary transport design is not solely about travel, but also about lifestyle.

BAD BOYS AND GIRLS SIT AT THE BACK; GRANNIES SIT AT THE FRONT; AND EVERYONE ENJOYS THE PANORAMA OF THE TOP DECK.
NICK TALBOT

BUSES

Created by a team led by industrial designer Douglas Scott and bus engineer Albert Arthur Durrant, the **ROUTEMASTER** bus became an international icon. Designed with mass-production in mind, it employed a modular system, constructed from the maximum number of interchangeable parts. It demonstrated that it is possible for a user-friendly vehicle to function properly and be well maintained. As designer Rodney Kinsman points out, the Routemaster was 'the last purpose-designed bus for London, designed to last, be repaired and accommodate change'.

In 2005, some fifty years after it first served the people of London, the much-loved bus was removed from the streets of the capital due to European Union legislation for disabled access. It is unfortunate that the low-floor replacements are yet to reach the design standards set by Scott, with interiors so badly designed that it is difficult to get a pushchair or wheelchair through them unless you enter through the back door.

Today, Transport for London favours the larger scale, single-floor options that are arguably less suited to the density of a city like London. Its fleet of bendy-buses, articulated and elongated vehicles, enable one-man operation and may improve health and safety, but they do little to improve passenger morale. The human face of public transport in the form of the friendly conductor is still the preferred choice of most passengers, especially tourists.

Bus travel is a social experience. Nick Talbot points to the different experiences in different parts of the vehicle: 'Bad boys and girls sit at the back; grannies sit at the front; and everyone enjoys the panorama of the

**ROUTEMASTER BUSES
AT CLAPTON DEPOT**
Photograph: Joe Kerr
2005

Filip Krnja/ Vehicle Design

F. Krnja 05

NEW ROUTEMASTERS FOR LONDON 2012
Design: Filip Krnja and Chan Chan whie Park
Vehicle Design, Royal College of Art
2005

top deck.' Post 9/11 and 7/7, issues of security concern many travellers and Talbot points out that 'it is now technically possible to have an explosive sniffer at the door of every bus'.

Dedicated bus ways offer a key to timetables, consistent operation, less energy, lower cost, customer satisfaction and increased use in urban environments, while fixed track, rapid transit remains an ideal option for the longer journey.

Bus design currently remains miles behind the innovations of private vehicles. There are a few exceptions, such as the FTR StreetCar pioneered by First plc and the Wright Group, and designed by Paul Blair. This solution runs along clearways, set-aside road space alongside public carriageways that is only for the use of public service vehicles. In theory this enables buses to run on time, but clearly such rapid bus-transit systems can only work if the infrastructure to support them is in place across the entire route. Thankfully, timetabling information sent by mobile phone should keep passengers informed of real-time locations. Inside, the StreetCar's atmosphere is more living room than bus, with cushioned recesses for the parent and child-buggy, and a gently curving 'sofa' of connected seats. The bus driver has kerb vision from the low-slung panoramic screen, complete protection within a locked compartment and two-way contact with his passengers via speaker-mikes and CCTV.

Onboard bus designers are experimenting with graphics, video facilities and computer linkage to access the Web – so perhaps Shillibeer was onto something with his on-bus library, albeit two centuries too soon.

STREETCAR RAPID BUS TRANSIT VEHICLE
Commission: First plc
Manufacturer: Wright Group
2005

PAY-AS-YOU-GO

If buses are currently a second-rate design option, perhaps shared car systems should bear more of the load. **STREETCAR** is a pay-as-you-go car club set up in London in 2004 and developing a multi-million pound business with 20,000 users predicted by 2009. Andrew Valentine, co-founder and Managing Director, suggests that StreetCar 'is now growing at a similar rate to more established schemes in the US and other parts of Europe'.

Users pay £4.95 an hour with fuel for up to 30 miles of driving, then 19 pence for each additional mile. Each car is activated by a smart card, with a pin number typed into an in-car keyboard, which releases an immobilizer under the bonnet; the keys are in the glove compartment, and the cars have names like Walt, Kylie and Ursula. There is even a Streetcar named Desire.

INFORMATICS

Information, particularly advanced journey information, is very important for reassuring passengers who have elected or been forced not to drive themselves. We are increasingly dependent on digital systems and capable of accessing travel data from our own mobile units. Such systems encourage journey planning and shift power from provider to user, something design is aiming for across the public transport spectrum.

Chiltern Railways has developed what it calls the Nomad system to access timetables and train-running information by Java-enabled mobiles (the ones with a joystick). Systems development has also already seen Transport for London adopt the Oyster ticket technology, where swipe cards (similar to those employed in New York) record user journeys and debit your account. It meets the principal objectives of a ticketing system: reduced fraud, faster access, simpler processing, less staff and fare flexibility. The system could embrace congestion and parking charges, and be extended to rail and river, not only in London, but nationwide.

SOCIAL CHANGE

Two recent projects at the Helen Hamlyn Research Centre have explored the complex social and environmental possibilities of bus travel.

Consultancy Capoco designs passenger vehicles for world markets and commissioned Helen Hamlyn Research Associate Merih Kunur to investigate, using a research matrix across spatial organization, social change and sustainability. 'We've considered the key drivers of change for the next twenty-five years – sustainable development, energy and emissions, access, information technology, integrated systems, safety, social factors and the cityscape itself,' comments Director Alan Ponsford.[23]

Ponsford sought 'an original statement about the future of mass transport', and Kunur delivered Mobilicity – a zero-emission, hybrid-electric, driverless vehicle system, running on global satellite-guidance sensors to fixed destinations. Designed from research in London, Hong Kong and Istanbul, the vehicles are low-floor, easy-access 12, 18, or 24-seaters, with flexible interior formulae for differing uses, and work singly or in platoons of up to six vehicles. According to Kunur, with his solution 'a greater sense of privacy is given to passengers, so this approach is socially as well as environmentally sustainable'.

Although mobility in cities remains the principal public transport challenge, the needs of rural communities have been addressed by another recent project at the Helen Hamlyn Research Centre. The bus manufacturer **OPTARE** and designer Owen Evans have come together to develop a multi-purpose country bus, which combines shop, library or surgery with passenger capacity. The bus can be fitted with the most appropriate kit for a particular journey or community. For rural communities and especially the elderly, already suffering from a loss of local amenities (largely due to the greater commuter distances that car drivers are willing to undertake), the bus offers a low-tech yet effective solution.

OPTARE ALERO CSV
Design: Owen Evans, Helen Hamlyn
Research Centre, Royal College of Art
Commission: Optare
2005

TROLLEYBUSES

The cross-over between bus and rail is the light railway or tram, originally horse-drawn, then electric, tyred as trolleybus, which is now making a comeback as an attractive light-track, fixed-route option in busy cities. In Hanover, Germany, Jasper Morrison's Ustra design updates the 1970s' Herbert Lindinger original, itself borrowing heavily from the Routemaster.

The Volvo Marcopolo articulated trolleybus is in service in São Paulo, Brazil, where 450 270-passenger vehicles are replacing an existing fleet with true zero emission at twice the efficiency of on-board electric motors. Articulated bus deployment is at its most innovative with Irisbus, using an optical guidance system and diesel-electric power in Rouen, France, and Las Vegas, while an articulated hybrid serves Eindhoven in Holland, utilizing liquid gas and electric-wheel motors.

BOMBARDIER's Guided Light Transit, Ansaldo-Breda's Stream and other guided bus systems parallel tramways in capacity, but need more space if slightly less infrastructural cost. They foreshadow a return to the trolleybus – a rubber-wheeled vehicle with electric traction from overhead wires, buried strips or other, similar power and guidance sources. The Guided Light Transit has already been built and tested.

BLADERUNNER
This dual-mode vehicle runs on road as well as rail and is applicable to freight and passenger transport
Design: Carl Henderson, Silvertip Design
2006

RAIL RALLIES

Britain's commuters might be forgiven for thinking that railways remain in the dark ages of post-Victorian development, with track repairs, signal failure and fatal accidents resulting from poor management. Elsewhere, France has the impressive SNCF; the link between Chep Lap Kok Airport and Hong Kong is well served by the AEL train; and the Japanese boast on-time systems and bullet trains. In the UK, the recent catalogue of rail disasters and fatal accidents has been most unfortunate, particularly at a time when national and local government is encouraging people to get out of their cars and catch the train. Again, the problem is twofold: the infrastructure, the tracks and the stations pose long-term issues and demand massive investment to upgrade, while the rolling stock is limited and often out of date.

Paul Priestman and his colleagues Nigel Goode and Ian Scoley have designed most modes of travel, from trains to aircraft, and are still excited by the design challenges on the move. Priestman has for a long time campaigned to improve standards of transport design and is disappointed that here in twenty-first century Britain we are still travelling in trains with slam-shut doors. He has demonstrated that trains should be more suited to the modern traveller. Priestman Goode's work for Richard Branson's Virgin Trains has proved a success with operators and passengers. Priestman set out to restore the romance of rail travel, providing travellers with private space through innovative detail design in standard class seating, plug-in facilities and folding tables.

Seymour Powell have designed 150 new vehicles with Bombardier Transportation for Midland Mainline; these reflect consumer research in their hotel-like interiors. First-class seats have shoulder and head supports for armchair privacy and comfort – the first all-leather British train seat. Standard interiors use colour, lighting and seat form to promote calm, and seats form a padded bench for children to lie down on. Vestibules and corridors use variable lighting to help the disabled and to introduce an element of 'theatre', and the bar imitates a patisserie or coffee bar. The design consultancy also worked on a fleet of innovative train forms that demonstrate the true potential for futuristic train designs. At present, as Paul Priestman laments, 'the design parameters for new British trains are severely restricted by train infrastructure, cost and legislation'. In 2004, Link Engineering and London and Continental Railways built Britain's first new railway for 100 years – the 300-kilometre-per-hour, 46-mile Eurostar link to London.

THE DESIGN PARAMETERS FOR NEW BRITISH TRAINS ARE SEVERELY RESTRICTED BY TRAIN INFRASTRUC- TURE, COST AND LEGISLATION
PAUL PRIESTMAN

In comparison, Japanese and Continental rail networks are offering greater capacity and other innovations, such as train carriages built from recyclable materials. The Shinkansen system, originating in the 1940s, first introduced in 1964 in Japan and extended in 1975, has long been regarded as a model of efficiency, speed and comfort. Scheduled to start service in 2007, new eight-car **SHINKANSEN** trains will link Shin-Osaka and Hakata, Japan, at speeds of up to 350 kilometres an hour. To reduce noise and wind resistance, the aluminium alloy vehicles will have 2 + 2 seating in standard class. The Tokaido and Sanyo Shinkansen sixteen-car trains will run up to 270 km/h on one route, 300 km/h on the other, using air-suspension tilting and a new digital automatic train-control system. These state-of-the-art trains take their name, Tokaido, from the feudal Eastern Sea Road from Kyoto to Tokyo, with its fifty-three stations offering lodgings, horses, porters and food for over 500 kilometres.

With Japan taking the lead and Continental systems not far behind, Britain is facing up to decades of investment neglect. According to Rodney Kinsman, 'We now have the opportunity for a train travel renaissance as trains are often the most direct route from city centre to city centre or airport to city centre.' As he points out, 'In the UK we still have slam doors, not in France, Spain, and now Italy; the Chinese for over thirty years have recognized that the train is the sensible and civilized way of travelling.'

In 1983, an airport link was pioneered at Birmingham, using Maglev (electro-magnetic levitation above a guideway rail). In China, Shanghai's Transrapid Maglev line at Pudong Airport is now exploring the same technology again. A five-car train set on the **YAMANASHI** Maglev Test Line has leading cars designed in three styles – aero-wedge, double cusp and the new MLX01-901, to minimize aerodynamic resistance. The airport link covers 30 kilometres in eight minutes at speeds of up to 267 miles an hour, compared to the road trip from Shanghai, which takes an hour.

Premier Zhu of China and Chancellor Schroeder of Germany inaugurated trials for the 2004 system. Premier Zhu noted that this was 'a major event in the history of Shanghai's urban development, as well as of China's railway transportation'. Siemens and ThyssenKrupp form part of the Transrapid consortium, which plans a 200-kilometre line from Shanghai to Hangzhou and a 1,250-kilometre link between Shanghai and Beijing – trains that virtually fly.

WE NOW HAVE THE OPPORTUNITY FOR A TRAIN TRAVEL RENAISSANCE AS TRAINS ARE OFTEN THE MOST DIRECT ROUTE FROM CITY CENTRE TO CITY CENTRE OR AIRPORT TO CITY CENTRE.

RODNEY KINSMAN

UP IN THE AIR

Flight today offers stark contrasts in passenger comfort, from the no-frills EasyJet phenomenon to the late-lamented Concorde. We are travelling further and further and more and more. Yet the true cost of our desire to work, explore and enjoy the world cannot be measured in financial terms, for it is the environmental costs that create the longer-term problems. Air travel is a massive pollutant in terms of both fuel and noise.

As more people opt out of the package-tour market, price-sensitive airlines may change and business trade is rapidly doing so, with more comfort, more facilities and much more design awareness. Inside the plane, design is already making changes and, similar to train travel, many designers in this field talk about trying to restore the glamour of travel and improve the time spent inside the cabin. Designer Tom Karen reminisces: 'Pre-war flying was slow and expensive but oh, so civilized – no check-in queues, no dreaded overhead bins, toilet discreetly located, social seating round tables, beautifully served meals and the captain came round to ask if you were enjoying your flight.'

The domain of design for flight has many practical and economic limitations. According to Paul Priestman, 'Aircraft seats are far more sophisticated than car seats, costing $40–100,000 each.' He continues, 'Distance between seats is a mathematical equation – the further apart the more comfortable, but the more expensive the ticket.'

THE QUEEN'S FLIGHT
Collage: Tom Karen
2002

DESIGNER AIRCRAFT

Designer Marc Newson has been obsessed with aircraft since childhood: 'I loved that planes took you to faraway places; they were streamlined and inherently beautiful. Air travel was as close as the average person could get to an out-of-this-world experience.'

Business class equates comfort with convenience, and Newson's Qantas Skybed, a seat which folds into a fully flat bed, includes innovative hoisting handles, a water-bottle container and a focused reading light. 'Most airline seats look like a collection of elements designed by different people. This is a coherent design.' The Qantas brand continue their collaboration with their preferred designer, who has designed a fleet of the new Airbus A380 'Super-Jumbo' and First Class lounges at Sydney and Melbourne airports.

Newson's contemporary design for the **DASSAULT FALCON 900B** is also coherent, using bold colour to enhance the feeling of space in the cabin, which is fitted out with chunky leather seats and clad with unusual carpet.

KELVIN40 CONCEPT JET
Design: Marc Newson
Commission: Fondation Cartier pour l'art contemporain
Photograph: Daniel Adric

DASSAULT FALCON JET 900B
Design: Marc Newson
Photograph: Tom Vack

For the **KELVIN40** concept jet, Newson had free reign to realize his sci-fi inspired fantasies. He set out to create a 'fictional aircraft', as urban theorist Paul Virilio described it, optimizing aerodynamics. This is a single-seater jet with aluminium fuselage, acrylic cockpit canopy, carbon-fibre wings and tail stabilizers 27 feet long and 7 feet high, with a 26-foot wingspan. The concept was commissioned and produced by Fondation Cartier pour l'art contemporain in Paris. Thus radical aircraft design sits more happily in the field of contemporary art than that of design.

Paul Priestman knows a great deal about design for aircraft, having worked for many leading airlines. Priestman identifies that the 'fixed design perimeters for aircraft design, are weight, fire, crash test and certification of use as passenger airline (criteria which are different from private jet requirements)', and explains that working for the airline industry 'we are branding these companies in a way that is tangible to the consumer'. His studio is currently working on fit-outs for a number of fleets of **AIRBUS A380** aircraft, having designed the first-class interior for the original new plane. The task was to present 'a vision of what the future could be' – to show what is possible, to provide absolute luxury, super-first class.

The design challenge for this product-led fit-out was creating space and light and different sensory experiences, achieved by using materials which are unusual on aircraft. Priestman Goode had relatively free reign over interior planning, and they incorporated bars, social areas, library and shower. Unfortunately, not all the design dreams for this conceptual super-first class will be possible in the realized fit-outs, but now Priestman Goode have been commissioned to do the serial build for tip-to-toe environments for three airlines, Lufthansa, Malaysian Airlines and Qatar Airlines (in all classes).

Priestman Goode won the competitive pitch for the fit-out for Lufthansa's A380, against among others BMW, because their concept was chosen by customers. For Malaysian Airlines the brief was to create the first executive jet on board a 747, with everything Malaysian in terms of colours, textures and even the linen on the beds.

AIR TRAVEL WAS AS CLOSE AS THE AVERAGE PERSON COULD GET TO AN OUT-OF-THIS-WORLD EXPERIENCE.
MARC NEWSON

AIRTIME IS SLEEP TIME

For many, particularly long-haul business travellers, regular flights are an opportunity to work or rest before the next round of appointments. Their design priorities are to be able to work in privacy and to rest in comfort. Airlines are employing the best of the international design industry to create brand differentiation to attract these high-paying customers.

The sleeper seat pioneered by British Airways revolutionized air travel and now most of the major firms have such an option for long haul in first and business classes, but the competition for innovation remains intense.

Pearson Lloyd and Softroom have collaborated on the evolutionary **VIRGIN ATLANTIC UPPER CLASS SUITE** in the Softroom Boeing 747-400 Airbus A340-300 and 600. Virgin Atlantic's Head of Design Joe Ferry's vision was an 'air of natural glamour' achieved with onboard bar and an empathetic airport lounge waiting area.

VIRGIN ATLANTIC UPPER CLASS SEAT BECOMES A FULLY FLAT BED
Commission: Virgin Atlantic
2005

SKYBED BUSINESS CLASS SEAT
Design: Marc Newson
Client: Qantas Airways
2004

VIRGIN ATLANTIC UPPER CLASS SUITE BAR
Design: Softroom
Commission: Virgin Atlantic
2004

In the cabin lighting is softened, and changes from lavender at dusk to 'golden hour' at sunset. Seeking relaxed sociability, similar to lounging around a pool, Softroom turned the seats inwards, to achieve, as Oliver Salway observes, 'the right combination of privacy and congeniality', retaining seat numbers and Virgin Atlantic's seat-to-bed mode.

AIRBUS INTERIOR LIBRARY AND LOUNGE CONCEPT
Design: Priestman Goode
Commission: Airbus
2004

Interior aircraft design has tended to focus on getting the largest number of seats into a given space. Tom Karen of Ogle Design has spent a life-time designing for transport and forming particularly strong views about the failings of aircraft design, from the passenger's perspective. 'Clinging to a conventional fuselage does not make a lot of sense: the body does not produce lift, the under-floor cargo space is hardly ideal and lots of space is wasted above the ceiling.'

GLOW SEAT
New materials glow in the dark when
the fabric is charged with light.
Design: Sheila Clark (MA RCA/FRCA)
Sponsors: Ford, Lotus, Nissan, Bute Fabrics,
Loro Piana and Manciewicz

WELL-BEING SEAT
Made of fabric woven with sustainable
bamboo that contains honey pectin,
is anti-bacterial and impermeable to
UV rays and a second fabric with silver
content, again ant-bacterial, anti-static
and deflects electro magnectic rays.
Design: Shelia Clark (MA RCA/FRCA)
Sponsors: Ford, Lotus, Nissan, Bute Fabrics,
Loro Piana and Manciewicz

Karen's Air Cruiser II is an exemplar project addressing many of the key design issues, with a fuselage made up of three horizontal bubbles to produce lift, facilitating smaller wings, with 'everything accommodated in one wide, sensible space without waste'. Other design features include a wider than usual entrance door with ceiling windows, which has since been adopted in Boeing's 787, accessible floor-to-ceiling luggage space, eliminating overhead lockers, and a coffee/snack area at the back 'for socializing and stretching legs'. The now commonplace telephone and computer facilities and 'round the table seating for groups and families' demonstrate the needs that Boeing has independently researched and confirmed. Purpose-designed ladies and gents' toilets are also part of the vision.

People who buy air travel also live beneath flight paths. Cambridge University is working with MIT, Boeing and Rolls-Royce on the Silent Aircraft Initiative. The 2.3 million-pound project envisages a flying wing fuselage with four high, rear-mounted jets, where engine noise is shielded from the ground, and the plane has more lift, a steeper descent path, acoustic duct liners and variable jet nozzles. 'The idea is to tackle aircraft noise by taking a completely fresh look at aircraft design,' says project manager Paul Collins. The concept aims to drastically reduce engine exhaust and fan noise on take-off, and to limit the time it takes to land. With 3–4 per cent growth in air travel forecast by 2015, the team seeks 'noise disturbance around airports …no louder than ambient urban noise outside airport boundaries'.

The partnership also includes the Civil Aviation Authority, British Airways and the National Air Traffic Services. The first 250-seat design would be scaled up to 800 in commercial use, and one further option is to eliminate windows, reducing the need for structural surrounds, and therefore weight, power/distance ratios and fuel costs and pollution. Instead passengers would sit by virtual windows, with screens relaying exterior camera images. This practical solution enables a wider body, facilitating more legroom and seat width, but divorces the passenger even further from the experience of flying.

AIRBUS FIRST-CLASS BAR CONCEPT
Design: Priestman Goode
Commission: Airbus
2004

BELL HELICOPTER FIT-OUT
Design: Seymour Powell
2005

PRIVATE FLIGHT

The ultimate in passenger luxury is the private jet and the Avio consortium of BAE Systems, General Dynamics, Avidyne and Williams International, is developing the Ellipse 500, 'the most electronic and computerized aircraft the general aviation industry has ever seen', according to chief executive Vern Raburn.[24]

It reduces weight and cost, increases safety and reliability, and centres on a holistic system that 'knows' what the aircraft is doing, through two aircraft-integrated electronics units (AIUs). Either can run the plane and host its computers, which run sensor systems for fuel, engines and environment. They include autopilot, auto-throttle, yaw damper and roll boost, with flaps, landing gear and lighting. The system has its own fault detection, using contact breakers for reliability. Instrumentation is simplified in crystal displays and split screens, and includes weather, radar, navigation and radio, digital maps and synoptics. The pilot operates a cursor and A–Z keyboard. 'The overriding result is you have two ways of doing everything,' says Don Taylor.[25]

The **BELL HELICOPTER 427 1FR** is a product of a design partnership between Ogle Models and Prototypes and Seymour Powell – the latter designing the new interior, and OM+P moulding and machining sections, each using sophisticated software. The fuselage was cut and stripped, and a new aluminium skin was fitted. Equipment and furnishings were then installed, using leather, chrome, laminate and paint finishes, and incorporating mood lighting in the floor, roof, seats, handles and cockpit – and a DVD system. Seymour Powell continue to work with Bell and have developed a range of interior fit-out options to suit different functions, including an air ambulance.

Supersonic travel is back on the design agenda, with Rolls-Royce's development of a supersonic jet engine aimed at the corporate market. Supersonic business jets are also under development by Cessna, Sukhoi and Tupolev, looking to build ten-seaters flying at up to Mach 1.

LEISURE AND EXPLORATION

Today the possibilities for leisure and exploration are incredible. The most extreme possibilities are limited to the wealthy and the brave, and the environmental costs of the pleasures of the few will affect us all.

At the extreme of the flight industry, Cecilia Hertz, founder of Stockholm's Umbilical Design, is one of six among 8,000 engineers at Houston designing for commercial space travel. 'It's an exciting field that's allowed me to look at styling and colours in a more complex way than traditional design.' With the push towards private space flight, interiors will be 'radically different …using light and sound and fragrance so that people will focus on enjoying the experience rather than panicking. We're working with psychologists on this.'

The design for a returnable space vehicle concentrated simply on getting in and out; future space travel offers a different choice, between a home-like environment and 'a new language of architecture and design …because you might get homesick'. This is perhaps relevant to most vehicle design in our fast-moving age. She adds, 'No one has the answers yet but we're searching for them.'[26] Virgin are planning space-age travel and Paul Priestman is discussing designs for space holidays, considering everything from tickets to space suits.

Just as visionary is Frank Heyl's **AEOLUS** oblique flying wing concept. This visualizes a second-generation supersonic airliner matching 747 seat-mile costs, cutting flying time in half. With 600 passengers, a 150-metre wingspan, and advanced passenger and baggage handling, it breaks new ground by applying existing technology. The load is carried in the wing, with swivelling engine pods facilitating different flying angles. An asymmetric profile reduces sonic boom significantly. The wing holds three detachable bays, suitable for differing cabin configurations. Unloading is swifter as units can be detached and replaced and aircraft turnaround significantly improved. Passengers and baggage occupy an integral unit, available on arrival, railed into the cabin, simplifying passenger and luggage transfer times, inspection and control.

International airline interest suggests that this is a concept with credibility, addressing several significant operating and customer issues. Frank Heyl: 'Industrial design often relates to the way technology is integrated into existing products, which accordingly alters appearance – a process known as co-evolution. New technologies mean projects can be "new stylistically, but also operationally innovative".'

USING LIGHT AND SOUND AND FRAGRANCE SO THAT PEOPLE WILL FOCUS ON ENJOYING THE EXPERIENCE RATHER THAN PANICKING.
CECILIA HERTZ

NINETY DEGREES SOUTH
Concept for Antarctic exploration vehicle
Design: James Moon, Royal College of Art
2004

AEOLUS CONCEPT PLANE
Design: Frank Heyl, Royal College of Art
2004

Fluidic flight, without control surfaces, depends on remote-controlled air flows. BAE Systems and the Engineering and Physical Sciences Research Council have funded Flaviir (flapless air vehicle integrated industrial design) with 6.2 million pounds, to be developed at Manchester University under direction from Professor Paul Ivey of Cranfield University, with teams from another eight institutions. Initially aimed at robotic aircraft, the principles, if successful, would apply equally to passenger aircraft. Research centres on air blowing from the wing edge, jet thrust vectored by secondary air flows and multiple surface-located synthetic jets. 'No one has flown anything like this before,' says Phil Woods of BAE Systems Advanced Technology Centre.

The more intrepid traveller who wants to keep his feet on the ground but seeks something different might be interested in the **NINETY DEGREES SOUTH** concept vehicle by James Moon. Working with the British Antarctic Survey team, Moon designed a lightweight, twin track, snow-specific vehicle with a remote pathfinder to detect dangerous crevasses, which can be airlifted to the parts others cannot reach, specifically snowmobiles.

Intended for expedition and scientific use, the vehicle has attracted interest in the Alps and Asian tundra, and might well be the ideal ice-hire car for two, with its twin seats and equipment space. Rebecca Feiner writing in the Telegraph found it 'witty yet practical' and 'the first enclosed off-site vehicle' for Antarcticans.[27] Designer James Moon says that 'Ninety Degrees South is both minimal environmental transport and scientific tool.'

ON THE WATER

Despite the impressive design heritage of cruiser liners, package-holiday cruises remain popular holiday choices especially for the retired, but rarely progress in design terms. At the top end, exclusive private yachts offer privacy and comfort to astonishing degrees of luxury provided for wealthy clients by companies like Wally Yachts.

Until Jon Bannenberg presented a 40-foot Moreland cruiser at the 1963 London Boat Show, the 'style' of most motor yachts had been borrowed from sailing yachts of the nineteenth century. In essence they were highly conservative, reflecting the gentleman's club, with varnished wood, bronze equipment and 'back-stairs' passages for the domestic crew, just like a traditional London town house.

Bannenberg recognized a role for the designer beyond that of the naval architect, to establish the yacht's atmosphere. 'Everything about his designs mattered to him – the exterior geometry certainly; the symmetry of interior layouts absolutely; the shape of the vase to hold the anemones on the owner's deck, and how the anemones were arranged, just as much as anything else.' His vision created revolutionary designs for top-end travel and led to hundreds of commissions for some of the wealthiest clients in the world, including the design for Adnan Khashoggi's 281-foot yacht, Nabila, and Steve Forbes's The Highlander.

74-METRE MOTOR YACHT; EXTERIOR STYLING STUDY
Design: Bannenberg
2006

72-METRE MOTOR YACHT
Wheelhouse interior study
Design: Bannenberg
2006

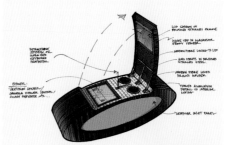

These mini-ships are complex spaces to redesign; they are unique packages constrained by many functional requirements. Now led by his son Dickie, **BANNENBERG DESIGN** has consistently tried to do something new and different, modernizing yacht design and redefining the possibilities for the interior and exterior spaces. Layouts maximize leisure and entertaining spaces and increasingly concentrate on bringing the users closer to the water and to the actual experience of yachting. This trend results in smartening up utility areas and lower decks (usually dominated by garages), improving swim platforms and increasing the size of the wheelhouse to enable more owner interface.

Creative Director Simon Rowell recognizes the trend for the wheelhouse to become 'a show-off space where owners like to bring their guests. Contemporary wheelhouses can be high-tech Star Wars-like environments, but many are still "yo ho ho and a bottle of rum" with the highest technology cocooned in brass and mahogany. Although equipment is getting smaller, new technology takes up the same or more space as increasingly advanced displays disseminate increasingly detailed information.' Dickie Bannenberg recognizes that 'Yachts are getting bigger and there is increasing diversification of yacht types – such as the explorer yachts, equivalent of off-road vehicles, enabling the more adventurous owners to go to different seas.'

110-METRE MOTOR YACHT;
BEACH CLUB INTERIOR CONCEPT
Design: Bannenberg
2006

YACHTPLUS 40 SIGNATURE SERIES BOAT FLEET
Design: Foster and Partners
Commission: YachtPlus UK
2005

David Nelson, Deputy Chairman of Foster and Partners, acknowledges that 'the joy of travelling by yacht is to be free on the water, to travel independently, to be able to reset course, be tremendously private or in some bubbly place'. Travelling by private yacht is tremendously relaxing for those lucky enough to experience it – it is not active sailing but more like an exclusive or bespoke hotel atmosphere.

The first yacht Foster and Partners worked on was Izanami, a 58.5-metre private vessel with a superstructure that was a radical departure from tradition. The naval architect died early in the design process, so Foster's role grew from fit-out to superstructure. The result remains the largest aluminium hull to be built to date, with hull and superstructure together forming a semi-monocoque construction of welded skin, frames and longitudinal stiffeners.

Since Izanami Foster's have turned down a few potential yacht design commissions, until **YACHTPLUS** offered the opportunity to design a fleet of boats for a range of owners (who together fund the development and running of the vessels in a shared ownership scheme similar to NetJets). In exchange for a share in a specific yacht, owners acquire year-round access to a fully crewed and serviced fleet of contemporary-designed, luxury motor yachts in both the Mediterranean and Caribbean. The design of the yachts prioritizes deck space (which is much greater than for other boats of similar scale). The boats have forward viewing cabins and a range of design features that enable customization to suit the wishes of multiple owners.

THE JOY OF TRAVELLING BY YACHT IS TO BE FREE ON THE WATER, TO TRAVEL INDEPENDENTLY, TO BE ABLE TO RESET COURSE, BE TREMENDOUSLY PRIVATE OR IN SOME BUBBLY PLACE

DAVID NELSON

YACHTPLUS 40 SIGNATURE SERIES BOAT FLEET
Design: Foster and Partners
Commission: YachtPlus UK
2005

At Fosters, David and his team have over the years designed many environments for travel, from bus shelters (for JCDecaux) to petrol stations (for Repsol), which do not neatly categorize into the practice's usual architectural work. Nelson believes that 'We are able to bring fresh eyes to this unique field of design by asking questions and challenging established traditions, in essence employing our usual means of analysis and methodology. Yachts are not really architecture or product design – they are a different world.'

WAIT–POINTS OF INTERCHANGE

START AND FINISH ARE PART OF THE JOURNEY; SO IS ANY INTERCHANGE.

Start and finish are part of the journey; so is any interchange. Travel is not just about vehicles – buildings matter before, during and after the journey. Successful public transport requires clean, light, safe, comfortable and informative terminals.

The vehicles we travel in on land and sea, and in the air, are entirely dependent on infrastructure, principally airports, bus depots, ferry terminals, railway stations, roads, car parks and petrol stations. Engineers and architects strive to match buildings and access, vehicles and people, technology and communication.

As the capability of vehicles increases, distances and regularity of travel increase, journeys get longer and inevitably there is more waiting time. Whether in cars waiting on over-trafficked motorways, in queues for tolls, in congested urban streets, or in public transport interchanges waiting for trains, buses or planes, we are held in places not of our choosing as we wait to move on.

The static passenger experience has become a determinant of transport choice. Buildings designed to connect people on the move are expanding beyond their purpose, seeking to blend commercial opportunity with aesthetic appeal and customer satisfaction.

Transport architecture lasts a long time, while vehicles change quickly. The fixed environments for transport are in many senses not as modern as the vehicles they greet. Plane technology has overtaken terminal technology, and cars are far more sophisticated environments than the car parks they rest in and the petrol stations where they refuel. Buildings are bespoke, long-term environments crafted together to suit individual requirements of site, geography, culture and cost. Manufactured moving objects, meanwhile, are designed with the absolute accuracy necessary for successful mass production and to a high standard of lifestyle expectation on a short-term life cycle.

HONG KONG INTERNATIONAL AIRPORT, CHEP LAP KOK
Design: Foster and Partners
1998

CITY TO CITY

Airport locations such as Stansted (London), **CHEP LAP KOK** (Hong Kong), Malpensa (Milan) and Roppongi (Tokyo) are moving further and further from city centres, resulting in longer door-to-door journey times. Any analysis of journey time in infrastructure time brings the train back into play – city to city or city to airport.

In the UK the Channel Tunnel connects Waterloo Station (by Sir Nicholas Grimshaw) to Paris's Gare du Nord at speeds that make the train competitive with the plane to Charles de Gaulle. No airport waiting time, no surplus journey time on the Heathrow Express – the train truly competes with the airline.

This example demonstrates the increasing demand for more and better facilities, whether rail or air or bus, with activities associated with work and leisure, so that the wait is an engaging experience as part of the whole business of movement. If we have to stop, we want good food, attractive shops, maximum information, minimum disruption, private space in public places, and an overall ambience that adds to, rather than diminishes, the travel experience. We do not want dank, dark platforms with flickering monitors and surly staff as we interchange between train routes; we do not want never-ending queues around those post-and-tape labyrinthine check-ins as we manhandle our baggage at airports; and we do not want cold and draughty waiting rooms with harsh (if any) seating, and dingy toilets with cracked tiles.

EXPO STATION, SINGAPORE
Design: Foster and Partners
2000

EXPO CATALYSTS

13 PLATFORMS FOR D-SOUTH URBAN RAIL LINE, HANOVER
Design: Desprang Architectken
2000

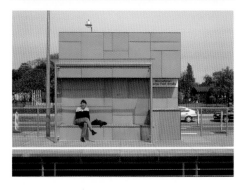

On the Scottish mainland, architect Nicoll Russell Studio's **DUNDEE BUS INTERCHANGE** Terminal uses thirteen Web-based route-finding terminals around the centre, 'bringing confidence into public transport'. **HANOVER EXPO** in 2000 was another key catalyst for transport infrastructure projects – its thirteen urban-rail platforms and waiting facilities for the new D-South urban rail line serving the exhibition were the outcome of a competition scheme, won by Desprang Architectken, Hanover. The line now serves new and existing districts, where the different materials used for the waiting blocks influence passengers' perceptions of time and space.

Railway stations, like airports, are often the first buildings that people experience when arriving in a city, and they therefore have an important symbolic role as urban gateways. Singapore's Expo Station, by Foster and Partners (1997–2001), is the first mass rapid-transport station that visitors to the city encounter when travelling along the new Changi Line once they leave Changi Airport. Built to serve the new Singapore Expo Centre, the station's design is both a celebration of arrival and a response to one of the warmest climates in the world.

The station is announced externally by two highly sculptural roof elements, which overlap to dynamic visual effect and appear to hover weightlessly above the concrete base. A 40 metre-diameter disc, clad in shining stainless steel, shelters the ticket hall and marks the station entrance, while a 130 metre-long, blade-like form, clad in titanium, covers the platforms, its reflective soffit constantly animated with the reflections of passengers and passing trains. The station is packed at peak times, so creating clear sight lines and a strong sense of orientation were fundamental to its design.

At ground level, the concourse is open, with views on one side to the street, and on the other side to a lush tropical garden created between the station and the Expo Centre. The elevated platforms are reached from the concourse and ticket office at street level by lift or escalators. Enclosure is kept to a minimum, and passengers can look up through a long cut in the floor structure to glimpse the trains overhead.

STATIONS

Certainly, the dirty station with vagrants is no longer acceptable. Stations henceforth must be clean and welcoming environments. In recent years we have seen Victorian stations improved, with major refurbishments at Paddington by Sir Michael Hopkins, and Kings Cross and St Pancras remodelled for the Eurostar. Likewise across the Atlantic, many American stations are being returned to their former glory, and re-established as sociable environments – places where you can eat and drink cocktails, such as the refurbishment of the romantic Oyster Bar at Grand Central Terminal, New York City, and SOM's scheme to reno-vate and extend America's busiest transportation facility, Pennsylvania Station, New York City, originally designed by legendary US architects McKim, Mead & White in 1900. Pennsylvania Station serves half a million people daily – more passengers than New York's three major airports combined, and more than twice the ridership of Grand Central Station.

The most exciting transportation project in New York City is Santiago Calatrava's work in Lower Manhattan. The rebuilding of the Ground Zero site provides a key opportunity to rethink the permanent urban transportation hub. This provides a service for the Port Authority Trans-Hudson commuter trains, New York City subway trains (1/9 E and N/R lines and a potential rail link to John F. Kennedy International Airport), as well as seamless, indoor pedestrian access to the World Financial Center, adjacent buildings, and the proposed new Fulton Street Transit Center. Calatrava has designed a freestanding structure of glass and steel, within a landscaped plaza.

In Germany, dominating the no-man's land where the Berlin Wall once stood, the city's Hauptbahnhoff literally towers over the capital – Europe's largest railway station, opened mid-2006, a symbol of united Germany. Eleven years in the building, the 'glass cathedral' fills a void in East-West infrastructure.

LYON-SATOLAS AIRPORT TGV STATION
Design:Santiago Calatrava
Photographs: John Edward

UNDERNEATH IT ALL

These examples of mass-transit interchange improvements are matched by Roland Paoletti's masterly design and engineering triumph for the Jubilee Line extension in London, linking Westminster to Stratford. Architect-in-charge of the twelve new stations Paoletti brought his experience from the Mass Transit Rail System in Hong Kong. Here for once architecture has leapt ahead of the vehicle. Ironically, the massive investment to update London's historic Tube system was also restricted by the technology of the original network. The result is journeys on rolling stock some forty years out of date, not air-conditioned, uncomfortable and difficult to maintain, running through tunnels of modern construction to stations of the twenty-first century. Paoletti's vision to commission different world-class architects for each station put architecture on a par with engineering, instead of allowing engineers to reduce the architecture to wallpaper.

The result of this fusion between architecture and engineering has created some of the most dramatic public buildings in London. The concourse at **CANARY WHARF STATION** by Foster and Partners has been compared to a cathedral. The curved glass canopies bring daylight from surface to platform some 25 metres below, and demonstrate the practice's marriage of form and function, also evidenced in its series of stations for Spain's Bilbao Metro Line 1.

CANARY WHARF STATION, JUBILEE LINE, LONDON
Design: Foster and Partners
2000

CONCEPT FOR OLYMPIC PODS FOR STRATFORD
LONDON, 2012
Design: Leslie Lau, Royal College of Art
2005

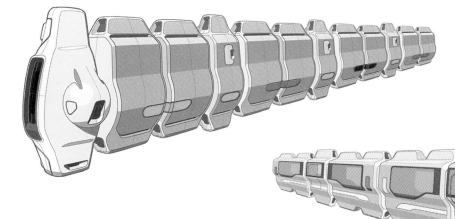

OLYMPIC OPPORTUNITY

Such connections between infrastructure and vehicles are vital to the well-being of cities and central to the way they are perceived. London's successful bid for the 2012 Olympic Games was undoubtedly influenced by the efficient, well-designed transport system already established to Stratford from Central London, where Eurostar terminals could bring passengers from Europe, and London's four airports could deposit international travellers.

Planning for the 2012 Olympics presages similar change and innovation in the long-term Lee Valley development, steered in part by transport needs. Already talented designers are pitching designs aimed at utilizing the waterways of the district and introducing new-style short-haul rail links for products and people, while patriotic and commercial interest is accelerating London Underground's efforts to service the expected inflow of overseas and British spectators.

It is not novel for investment in transportation infrastructure to be prompted by significant events such as the Olympic Games. In Munich in 1972, the prospect of millions of Olympic visitors from around the world provided a new impetus. Ahead of schedule, the first subway line, the U3/6 from Goetheplatz to Kieferngarten, opened in 1971. The history of the Munich transport system is relatively young. After the Second World War and a thwarted first attempt at a subway system, it took another two decades, prolonged disputes between city and Bundesbahn (German Federal Railway) and hopelessly congested streets before, in 1965, construction of the Munich subway began. At present the Bahn system has 92 kilometres of rail with ninety stations.

With a strong track record in urban regeneration projects, as well as small-scale works such as pedestrian bridges and schools, architects Auer + Weber were commissioned by Munich City to design the subway station at **WESTFRIEDHOF** as part of an ongoing and enlightened procurement of outstanding architecture for key subway stations. Above ground the new station that services the new U1 line consists of a lightweight, transparent glass and steel structure that accommodates an interchange between bus and U-Bahn transport modes.

Descending the escalators to platform level, the space is more reminiscent of a lighting installation than a transportation hub. Designer Ingo Maurer, who is renowned for his conceptual approach to lighting design, collaborated with Auer + Weber to create the dramatic interior. A row of eleven large-scale aluminium hemispheres, each with a diameter of 3.8 metres and housing twelve fluorescent tubes, is suspended over the column-free station. Plans for an obscured-glass lining to the concrete structure were abandoned in order to bring out the true nature of the hammered concrete tunnel areas.

Similarly, the twenty-ninth Olympiad, to be held in China in 2008, has required massive transportation infrastructural change. Beijing's new international airport terminal by Foster and Partners has been designed as the gateway to the city, welcoming athletes from around the world.

WESTFRIEDHOF SUBWAY STATION, MUNICH
Design: Auer + Weber with Ingo Maurer
Photographs: Angelo Kaunat

TOMORROW'S AIRPORT

Beijing has the world's largest and most advanced airport building – not only technologically, but also in terms of passenger experience, operational efficiency and sustainability. Its soaring aerodynamic roof and dragon-like form celebrate the thrill and poetry of flight and evoke traditional Chinese colours and symbols.

Although conceived on an unprecedented scale, the design for Beijing expands on the new airport paradigm created by Foster in the early 1990s at Stansted Airport. That project turned the traditional section of an airport upside-down, elevating the passenger concourse from the ground plane and putting a clear span roof over the top, enabling flexibility and views through to aircraft. With this design, passenger connectivity to aircraft was transformed.

Designed for maximum flexibility to cope with the unpredictable nature of the aviation industry Beijing, like its predecessors at Stansted and Chep Lap Kok, aims to resolve the complexities of modern air travel, combining spatial clarity with high service standards.

Between the existing eastern runway and the future third runway, the terminal encloses a floor area of more than a million square metres, designed to accommodate some forty-three million passengers per annum, rising to fifty-three million by 2015. Public transport connections are fully integrated, walking distances for passengers are short, with few

BEIJING AIRPORT, CHINA
Design: Foster and Partners
2008

changes of level, and transfer times between flights are minimized. Like at Chep Lap Kok, the terminal is open to views to the outside under a single, unifying roof canopy, whose linear skylights are both an aid to orientation and sources of daylight – the colour cast changing from red to yellow as passengers progress through the building.

The terminal building will be one of the world's most sustainable, incorporating a range of passive environmental design concepts, such as the south-easterly oriented skylights, which maximize heat from the morning sun, and an integrated, eco-friendly environment-control system. Remarkably, it will have been designed and built in just four years.

Another British architectural practice to benefit from the Beijing Olympics is Terry Farrell and Partners, with its winning competition entry for a railway station at **BEIJING SOUTH**. The design incorporates a roof over 500 metres long. The brief also required an intermodal passenger interchange between metro, bus, car and taxi transport. The design and master plan of the scheme creates an urban link with the surrounding cityscape. A landscaped pedestrian axial spine maximizes the sense of approach and creates public spaces to integrate the station within the urban fabric.

SUPER CITY STATION

KOWLOON STATION, Hong Kong, with its master-plan 1,100,000 square metres of mixed-use space associated with the station, was part of a plan instigated in 1989 by the Hong Kong government, to replace its congested airport at Kai Tak with a new 12 billion dollar airport on the manmade island of Chep Lap Kok. The airport by Foster and Partners is linked to Hong Kong Central by a sophisticated road and high-speed rail corridor.

Designed by Terry Farrell and Partners, Kowloon Station is the first experience of Hong Kong for millions of people. The concourse, with escalators, lifts and stairs connecting various modes, is a single space animated through passenger movement. Along the rail axis, thirty-four escalators and seventy-one staircases descend 14 metres through a grand escalator hall, from ground level to the Tung Chung MTR Line platforms at the station's lowest level.

BEIJING SOUTH STATION, CHINA
Design: Farrell and Partners

The design provides for passenger interchange between three separate rail links, airport check-in, and taxi and other local transportation. The concept behind Kowloon Station, a project that incorporates all urban systems in one giant web, is today's supremacy of urban connectivity. On a global level, the transport system provides a high-speed link to Chep Lap Kok Airport and the world beyond. On a micro level, the urban plan, driven initially by route planning within the station, ensures that this quarter of the city has superb internal connections.

KOWLOON STATION AND MASTERPLAN, HONG KONG
Design: Farrell and Partners
1998

Farrell was also successful with his competition entry for a new station at
GUANGZHOU, China, billed as the largest new station in Asia, consisting of
twenty-eight elevated island platforms and three underground metro lines.

China's new stations are intended to become platforms for compact city
districts linked by rail lines that will eventually form a 193-kilometre
integrated linear city, sweeping north as far as the mainland city of
Guangzhou, where the government programme of over 120 airports,
currently under development, reaches its climax with a vast airport
designed by American architects Parsons.

GUANGZHOU STATION, CHINA
Design: Farrell and Partners

TAKE A SEAT

Design for future movement is not limited to buildings, but extends to detail, such as seating, where the discerning – and often weary – passenger seeks rest and relaxation.

'Design for transport is all about addressing the brief and the focus of the brief should be about really understanding passenger need,' says Rodney Kinsman. If you have sat in a seat in a terminal in Africa, America, Europe, the Middle East or Asia, you will have experienced Kinsman's design. Since he established **OMK** in 1966, the company has supplied furniture for waiting in over a hundred airports, railways and ferry terminals worldwide. The constant commissions reflect the homogenization of international travel, yet also allow for cultural differences via an extensive range of modules, materials and colours. For the fit-out of Guangzhou Airport, 14,000 OMK seats in the finest finishes of leather and granite float above miles of marble flooring. In Finland's Helsinki-Vantaa Airport, 1,000 dark, leather-clad reclining seats with full headrests and footrests offer executive levels of comfort. On London's Jubilee Line, OMK's slick aluminium benches offer a place to perch while waiting a few moments for the Tube.

The longstanding success of OMK's furniture range reflects the demand for comfortable, durable and easy-maintenance seating. Trax public seating is a modular system, made up of interchangeable components mounted on an anodized aluminium beam, allowing the operator flexibility before and after installation.

As for all design for transportation environments, Kinsman works within tight parameters, determined by clients' wishes and budgets, safety legislation and fire restrictions (so no inflammable materials, and no loose seating that people could move). The size of the seat is predicated on the average size of the human behind, and the optimum time of use. Provision for seating is frequently limited, with perhaps 50 seats for every 4,000 people, whereas the priority should be passenger comfort – not to keep them on their feet, keep them walking. Thus there has developed a simple paradox – the need to maximize investment while facilitating transit, to utilize space while enhancing the experience, and to merge comfort and convenience with commercial opportunity for the pleasure of the traveller and to the profit of the facility.

TRAX SEATING DIAGRAM
Design: OMK
Original design: 1996

OMK SEATS AT HELSINKI-VANTAA AIRPORT
Design: Rodney Kinsman, OMK
2005

AIRPORT SHOPPING

As the wait becomes integral to travel, so the need to cater for passenger boredom becomes greater and the opportunity for retail widens. Today retail space is the biggest source of income for airports – bigger than travel itself.

The profit imperative within terminals conflicts with the customer's demand for more space, convenience and comfort and less intrusion, distraction and inconvenience. The answer is shopping, for in the retail zones the traveller can be seduced by lifestyle accessories and countless goodies crying out to be added to the journey, as part of the travel experience. While supplementary shopping is an appropriate commercial response to opportunity, the airport, as one commentator puts it, 'should be concentrating on the traveller, not trying to flog them stuff'.

In Terminal Architecture, Martin Pawley brilliantly records the evolution of the airport terminal as building type.[28] Terminals are complex buildings, where the airport function can itself be compromised, since they have in many cases become out-of-town shopping malls first, and places for travel second. Thankfully, designers are rising to the challenge and the quality of the shopping experience at some airports matches if not exceeds that of the high street. At Amsterdam's **SCHIPOL AIRPORT**, retail areas by London's Virgile and Stone see the design firm bringing the design standards they have demonstrated for luxury brands such as Burberry, Yves Saint Laurent and Space.NK within the central terminal. That level of quality is certainly expected by the British Airports Authority (BAA) for the retail units at their new terminal building at Heathrow, where rents and store incomes may well exceed that of Central London's most prestigious shopping streets.

SCHIPOL AIRPORT, AMSTERDAM
Retail design: Virgile and Stone
2000

TERMINAL 5 HEATHROW

With the growth of air travel, **TERMINAL 5** at London's Heathrow Airport is the current phase of airport expansion. Intended to reinforce Heathrow's position as Europe's principal intercontinental hub, the terminal to be used by British Airways was the subject of a design competition in 1989 won by Richard Rogers Partnership.

Client BAA and major tenant British Airways required a new terminal building and two satellite buildings on a site covering some 260 hectares (the terminal area alone is the size of fifty football pitches). This would be a complex capable of handling up to 35 million passengers a year, which would contribute less carbon emissions than the older buildings and contribute positively to its location.

The terminal itself, on the site of a former sewage-treatment plant to the west of the existing airport, includes the world's largest baggage-handling system, major airside retail facilities, large lounges and sixty aircraft stands. Ancillary components of the development include two satellite buildings, a hotel, a new train station accessing London Underground and the Heathrow Express, coach and bus station, short-term parking facilities and a new spur road from the M25 motorway. In addition, the design has had to satisfy a large and diverse group of stakeholders, including 5,000 workers and 2,000 support staff, comprising security immigration, customs, retail tenants, public transport operators and local authorities.

TERMINAL 5, HEATHROW AIRPORT, LONDON
Design: Richard Rogers Partnership
Interiors: Priestman Goode
Client: BAA
2005

MOST
TERMINALS
CREATE A MUCH
BETTER
DEPARTURES
THAN ARRIVALS
JOURNEY
EXPERIENCE
DAVID BARTLETT

Rogers' winning design became the subject of a three-year public enquiry, focused on all proposed development at Heathrow. Feasibility work on the master plan and buildings continued, but final approval for the scheme was only granted over a decade later in 2003. Richard Rogers' office was also commissioned to design a new air-traffic control tower, to provide a state-of-the-art platform for controllers at Heathrow.

The design team led by Mike Davies developed a roof with a loose fit, allowing the building envelope and the interior to absorb change without structural interference. A grand entrance between terminal building and forecourt/car-park building breaks the mould. High-level bridges across the space, and the vertical circulation core from the railway station, provide departing passengers with a dramatic open and light-filled space for the transition from outside to inside. It is hoped that fifty per cent of all journeys to and from the terminal will be on public transport, so BAA 'had to look at the project as a whole multi-modal interchange, not just another terminal building'.

The concept was 'predicated on the whole physical and emotional experience of the passenger and their personal journey within the terminal', says BAA Head of Design for Terminal 5 David Bartlett. The design leads passengers through the building from arrival to departure in a logical and legible sequence, offering panoramic views and adding enjoyment to the airport experience. All passengers enter the building at

TERMINAL 5, HEATHROW AIRPORT, LONDON
Design: Richard Rogers Partnership
Interiors: Priestman Goode
Client: BAA
2005

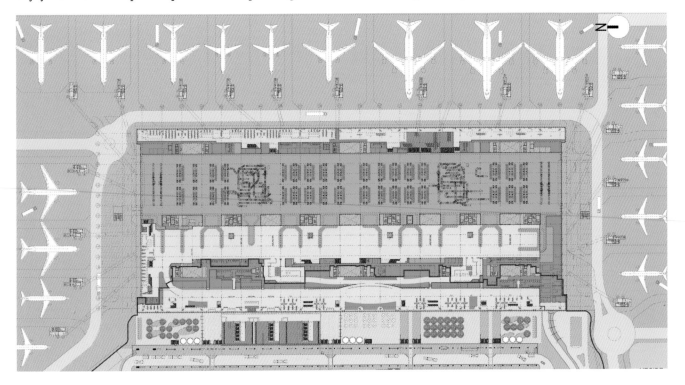

the same point on the western side of the departures concourse, regardless of how they reached it. 'Most terminals [create] a much better departures than arrivals journey experience,' says Bartlett. 'We have attempted to redress this imbalance by providing interesting spaces …dramatically lit …where passengers need a welcoming environment that facilitates their movement quickly and efficiently.'

For Terminal 5, Priestman Goode are 'concept guardians' for the interior products tasked with providing a coherent experience at all points in the passenger journey. They have created concept designs for all transactional points in the journey including three check-in 'waves' on the departures concourse: self service, fast bag drop and conventional check-in desks.

Bartlett recognizes that 'T5 has transformed Heathrow's brand and image,' adding that the wave-like roof silhouette and control tower 'are recognizable icons that herald an exciting new future for Heathrow as a gateway to Britain'.

TERMINAL 5, HEATHROW AIRPORT, LONDON
Design: Richard Rogers Partnership
Interiors: Priestman Goode
Client: BAA
2005

100–101

TERMINAL 5, HEATHROW AIRPORT, LONDON
Design: Richard Rogers Partnership
Client: BAA
2005

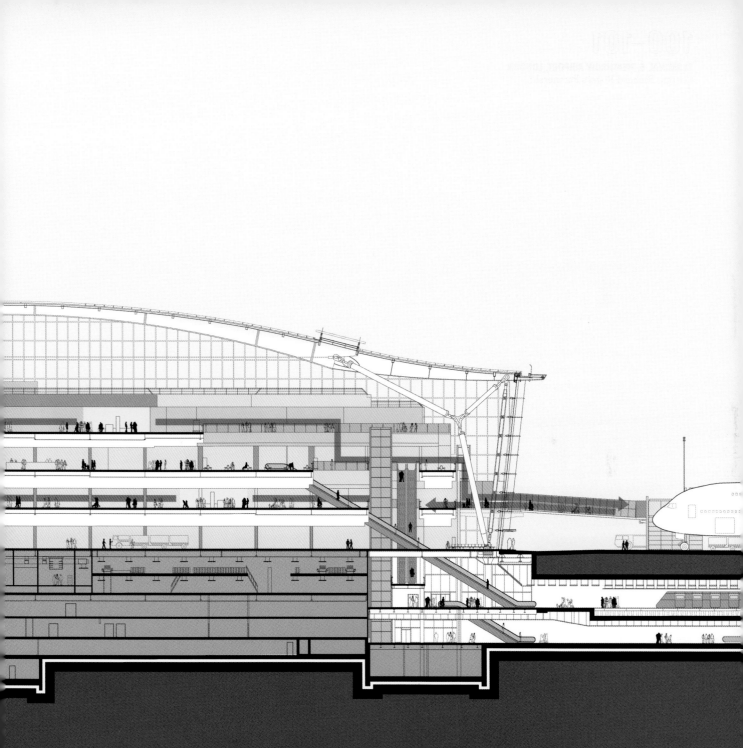

NEW EUROPEAN TERMINALS

MADRID BARAJAS AIRPORT, Spain, is the largest so far completed by the Richard Rogers Partnership – more than a million square metres of buildings with a budget of around a billion euros. The new terminal and satellite are designed to handle up to thirty-five million passengers annually, establishing Madrid as a major European hub.

The new terminal features a clear progression of spaces for departing and arriving travellers. The building's legible, modular design creates a repeating sequence of waves formed by vast wings of prefabricated steel. Supported on central 'trees', the great roof is punctuated by roof lights, providing carefully controlled natural light throughout the upper level of the terminal. Light-filled 'canyons' divide the parallel floors that accommodate the various stages of passenger processing – from point of arrival, through check-in and passport and security controls, to departure lounges and, finally, to the aircraft.

MADRID AIRPORT, SPAIN
Design: Richard Rogers Partnership
2005

MADRID AIRPORT, SPAIN
Design: Richard Rogers Partnership
2005

A simple palette of materials and straightforward detailing reinforce the direct character of the architecture. Internally, the roof is clad in bamboo strips, giving it a smooth and seamless appearance. In contrast, the structural 'trees' are painted to create a kilometre-long vista of graduated colour.

Spain's own Santiago Calatrava has built some of the most beautiful contemporary environments for waiting, including bus and train stations for the Lisbon Expo. At Bilbao Airport, Calatrava continues the design tradition started by the legendary Finnish architect Eliel Saarinen, with the bird-like TWA terminal at New York's JFK Airport. Calatrava's aerodynamic roof spans the administrative areas, creating areas where restaurants and waiting areas are located behind the canted glazed facades, directly overlooking the apron and runways.

UNDER AND OVER GROUND

A similar challenge to create a new civic landmark was also addressed for the **EUSKO TREN** in Durango, Spain, where Zaha Hadid worked with Patrick Schumacher to integrate a new underground station with the government's Basque transport headquarters. The dramatic design articulates Eusko Tren's new identity, continuing Bilbao's policy of well-designed transport infrastructure, started by Foster's Bilbao Metro of 1998 (and 2004), and reinforced by Calatrava with Sondica Airport terminal (1990–2000).

Foster's influence on railway design extends to Italy's new, high-speed rail network, for which the government has instituted a major programme of station restructuring and new-build. David Nelson, Deputy Chairman of Foster and Partners, explains that the challenge in designing the 2003 competition-winning scheme for **FLORENCE HIGH SPEED TRAIN STATION** was 'to bring something of the future to the history of Florence itself'. Nelson

NEW EUSKO TREN CENTRAL HEADQUARTERS, RAILWAY STATION AND URBAN PLANNING, DURANGO, SPAIN
Design: Zaha Hadid with Patrick Schumacher
Client: Department of Transport and Public Works of the Basque Government, Bilbao, Spain
2004

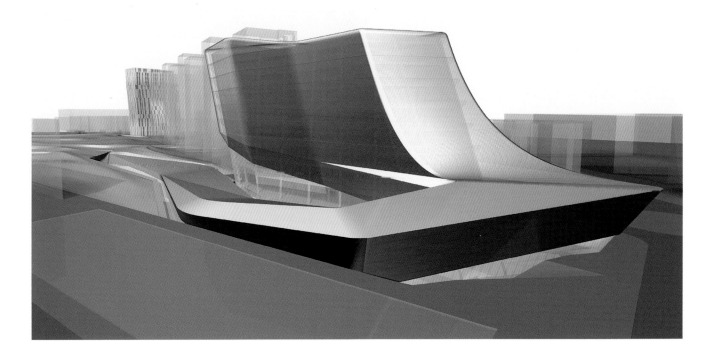

continues, 'We felt a tremendous responsibility to the classical city that has inspired so many others. The project brings the latest technology for train travel to the heart of the city, mixing old and new on a scale not tackled before.' Indeed, from design to build is a long time span; it could be ten years, but the building will last a long time. 'We felt the sense of history, designing today a contemporary station with natural light and photovoltaic cells, yet in this historical context the design has a degree of permanence, being classical, strong and emotive in a manner that ensures it belongs to Florence and can't be anywhere else.'

FLORENCE HIGH SPEED TRAIN STATION will be the point of arrival in the city for many people. The moment you get off the train, 25 metres below ground, you will feel you are in Florence because of the scale and drama of the space, reflecting the grandeur of the city. The station chamber consists of a single volume, 454 metres long and 52 metres wide, using cut-and-cover techniques similar to those at Canary Wharf. Passengers move from platform to ground level via lifts or escalators. Between the platform level and the street are two levels of shops, while a terrace at street level offers views and connectivity to the trains. The composition is

FLORENCE HIGH SPEED TRAIN STATION
Design: Foster and Partners
Client: RFI (Rete Ferrovia Italiana)
2003 – 2010

HIGH SPEED TRAIN STATION NAPOLI AFRAGOLA
Design: Zaha Hadid with Patrick Schumacher
Client: TAV s.p

capped by an arching glazed roof, which evokes the great railway structures of the nineteenth century. Natural light flooding in from above gives an immediate sense of space and light. From within the station one can see the sky and sense the city.

Conversely, Hadid and Schumacher have designed a bridge above the train tracks in Naples as part of their design for the **NEW HIGH SPEED TRAIN STATION NAPOLI AFRAGOLA**, scheduled to open in 2008. This concept emerged from enlarging the overhead concourse access to various platforms, so that it becomes the main passenger concourse itself. Providing an urbanized public link across the tracks highlights the new through-station, which also acts as the nucleus of a business park linking surrounding towns.

The bridge concept facilitates two strips of extended parkland alongside the tracks, opening and connecting the site to the surrounding landscape and business park. This expresses the articulation of movement, enhanced within the building, where the trajectory of travellers shapes the geometry of the space. Thus rather than reflecting its context, this station sits as a sculptural icon on the edge of the city.

HIGH SPEED TRAIN STATION NAPOLI AFRAGOLA
Design: Zaha Hadid with Patrick Schumacher
Client: TAV s.p.a.
2003 – 2008

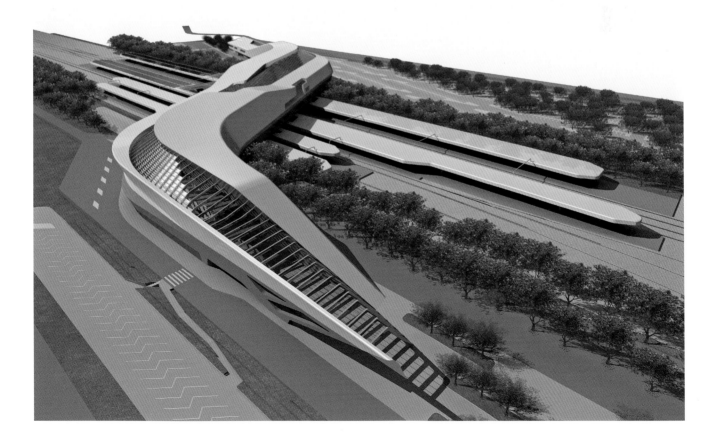

ALL AT SEA

Once the poor relation of the airports and stations, ferry terminals are now getting the design attention they deserve.

In **YOKOHAMA**, Japan, the old harbour front, once a gateway for foreigners and goods alike, saw heavy industry moving from the city centre, and the waterfront developing commerce, entertainment and the need for a new ferry terminal. Foreign Office Architects (FOA) of London designed the new international passenger terminal. Husband and wife team Alejandro Zaera-Polo and Farshid Moussavi literally broke new ground with their complex roof design. The dramatic structure, made from a network of interconnecting surfaces, provides a parkland above and dramatic spaces within the terminal. Its spine, suggesting a ship form, linking land to sea, employs interlocking loops of folded steel resistant to earthquake stresses, blending the practical with the aesthetic.

Zaha Hadid's maritime ferry terminal at **SALERNO** in southern Italy forges a new, intimate relationship between city and water. Like an oyster, it has a hard shell that encloses soft, fluid elements. A 'nerved' roof acts as an

YOKOHAMA INTERNATIONAL PASSENGER TERMINAL, JAPAN
Design: Foreign Office Architects
2002

**YOKOHAMA INTERNATIONAL PASSENGER
TERMINAL, JAPAN**
Design: Foreign Office Architects
2002

extended protection against the intense Mediterranean sun. The site is
sculpted as a smooth hill upon which a sloped path begins. This whole
area is indicatively lit to guide passengers through the length of the
building, the glow of the terminal acting like a lighthouse to the port,
a symbolic mark on the complex Norman and Saracen city traces.

Functionally, the terminal is composed of three main interlocking
elements: offices for the administrative section, docks for the ferries and
harbour for the cruise ships. Daily ferry passenger movements are fast
and intense, and the ground plan enhances speed and efficiency. The
passenger will arrive, buy ticket, coffee and newspaper, ascend via
ramps to the upper level and reach the vessel entrance. The new terminal
will operate both visually and actively as an intensified, smooth transition
between land and sea.

MARITIME TERMINAL, SALERNO, ITALY
Design: Zaha Hadid Architects
Client: Comune di Salerno
2006

London's Thamesside waterscape changed radically with Marks Barfield's visionary London Eye, and was later supplemented by Tate Britain's Ferry Pier. The same architects have won the five million pound Isle of Wight ferry terminal design competition. **RYDE INTERCHANGE** is the main transport hub for the Isle of Wight. Intended as an iconic landmark, the interchange will improve overall access and create stronger physical and visual linkages between pier, esplanade and town centre, facilitating seafront tourism and leisure. Serving three million passengers annually, the design is unique in terms of modal mix – ferry, hovercraft, train, bus, taxi, coach, pedestrians and cyclists. The architectural 'form' takes inspiration from the landscape, in a visually striking design. The building will have a low environmental impact in construction methods, materials and use of resources.

On a British west-coast island, **TIREE** Art Enterprises invited Sutherland Hussey Architects to design a ferry-passenger shelter, next to the pier, for passengers crossing to the mainland. Funders Scottish Arts Council called for an artist, architect and engineer to collaborate throughout.

The Shelter, completed to budget (£598,000), is an exquisite building, responding to its environment. It interprets the rugged features of the island and essential site assets, such as the undulating stone dyke and underlying bedrock. Other elements, such as the large expanse of sea, horizon line, white quartz beaches and monochromatic black houses, all influenced three distinctive architectural elements. A white-walled corridor creates a linear cut in the landscape; the walls open to the elements, encouraging the user to focus on the sky. A black, open-ended wooden box provides a stark contrast to the corridor, moving the viewer from light to dark, from exposed to protected. The glass belvedere, which extends from the wooden box, provides a focal element for disembarking visitors. The glass roof collects rainwater and allows it to stream down the windows, heightening the weather experience.

TIREE FERRY TERMINAL
Design: Sutherland Hussey Architects
Photograph: Colin Harris

TIREE FERRY TERMINAL
Design: Sutherland Hussey Architects
Photograph: Donald Urquhart

SWISS STANDARD

The small Swiss town of **WORB**, at the end of the commuter line from Berne city centre, marks the entrance to the scenic Emmental region. Smarch Architects in collaboration with Conzett, Bronzini, Gartmann Engineers won the competition to design a new train station that incorporates a train depot and a covered car park. The car park, on the upper floor of the concrete slab and column construction, allows passengers to transfer straight to the station without going underground.

The constricted site, with its gently curved train tracks, informs the building's dynamic architecture. The walls of the outer shell comprise 130 metres of stainless-steel ribbons, held on cylindrical concrete columns by tension alone. The ribbons are clamped together in alternating spaces between the columns. The walls' reflections shift as passengers move through the station. At the same time, the horizontal structure of the strips keeps the building 'open, providing a deterrent to vandals while allowing sun and air to flow through'.

WORB STATION, WORB, SWITZERLAND
Design: Smarch Architects
2004

TRAFFIC NOISE

Noise is always a problem in the transport context; householders invest in triple glazing near motorways, and acoustic panels soften pedestrian clatter in terminals, while station announcers battle to be heard in busy concourses.

Kas Oosterhuis and IIona Lénárd faced the challenge of taming traffic roar along the A2 highway in Rotterdam, the Netherlands, when designing the Cockpit industrial building. This required combining a 1.5-kilometre acoustic barrier with 5,000 square metres of factory space. Cars, power-boats and planes are streamlined to diminish drag; the **ACOUSTIC BARRIER** and the Cockpit do not move themselves, but they are placed in a continuous flow of passing cars. This swarm streams by with a speed of 120 km/h along the acoustic barrier. The length of the building is ten times its height. The concept of the Cockpit was inspired by its integral namesake within the smooth body of a Starfighter. The building acts as a three-dimensional logo for the commercial area hidden behind the barrier.

Within the Cockpit, the Hessing showroom is immersed in the long, stretched volume of the acoustic barrier, striking for its use of continuous lines, without an explicit beginning and no abrupt end. Close to the Cockpit the top line ascends and the bottom line dips, creating the showroom space, a horizontal cathedral for cars. Hessing displays Rolls-Royce, Bentley, Lamborghini and Maserati, and beneath the spectacular 3D track of the showrooms the workshop and garage reveal the tops of cars under repair.

A2 HIGHWAY, ROTTERDAM; HESSING SHOWROOM, A STREAMLINED COCKPIT ACOUSTIC BARRIER
Design: Kas Oosterhuis and IIona Lénárd
2005

PARK AND LIGHT

Zaha Hadid's first realized transportation project was the car park and terminus at Hoenheim North, **STRASBOURG**, France. The city introduced a second cross-city line, inviting Hadid to design the tram terminus for Line B to encourage 'park and ride', to combat pollution and congestion.

The station's function is basic – waiting space, bicycle storage, toilets and a shop. The play of lines mapped out at ground level is projected on to the lighting datum in the floor, furniture, architecture and strip lights in the ceiling. The overall effect is that of a dynamic and energetic space, the lines joining to create fluidity.

The car park is divided in two parts to cater for 700 cars. White lines align on the north-south axis at the lowest point, and then gently shift according to the curvature of the site boundaries. Each parking space is marked by vertical light posts, which create a field of light while keeping a constant datum height as the ground level gradually slopes. The architecture presents a new urban landscape and a bold civic gesture.

The overall concept visualized an integrated structure or series of fields with no clear delineations between car park and station. The concept of seamless physical transition between functions was directly applied to the architecture. The so-called fields represent the patterns of movement of cars, trams, bicycles and pedestrians, each mapping a particular trajectory.

CAR PARK AND TERMINUS MULTIMODAL
HOENHEIM NORD, STRASBOURG, FRANCE
Design: Zaha Hadid Architects
Client: Communaute Urbaine de Strasbourg
2005

FILL 'ER UP

Finding fuel in an attractive environment was once a feature of British byways, and a magnet for original design on the Continent and in the USA, attracting designers such as Raymond Lowey for Shell and BP, and Eliot Noyes for **MOBIL**. As a result of the ascendancy of global oil companies and the desire, if not the need, to standardize, petrol and service stations have acquired a dull monotony, and a monolithic rectilinear canopy complete with obligatory low-profile retail shed. Motorway service stations are no better, with their suburban, red-brick villa-esque profiles.

Foster and Partners' stations for Spanish oil company Repsol redefine the single canopy as a series of inverted kites or pyramids, standing out in the landscape in the company's bold brand colours of orange, red and white, contrasted with black.

European motorways boast breathtaking bridge structures and positive landscaping, as petrol stations compete for custom, seeking means to appeal through more sympathetic design. Samyn en Partners' twin petrol station at Wanlin in Belgium shelters beneath umbrella canopies of pre-stressed membranes, embracing the entire forecourt and integral shop. A diffuse light shines through the membrane, which echoes the hilly terrain, while sound reflection lends an extra ambience beneath the canopy.

By contrast, flowing form rather than local idiom is epitomized in Shoei Yoh's undulating roof for the filling station on the entrance road to Oguni, Japan, where four concrete arches of different heights and depths are linked by a steel and aluminium grid incorporating stainless-steel and laminated glass panels, offering a dramatic and enticing prospect.

As the developing world buys into automania, rural fuel stations may well be mobile in the first instance. On the outskirts of Kuala Lumpur, Malaysia, Petronas operate an Elf unit with a simple attached canopy on each side and above-ground tanks, not unlike the Agip winged station temporarily based in Prague, Czech Republic, several years ago.

Equally, the gradual onset of alternative fuels predicates a need for electric charging stations, hydrogen filling stations and ethanol tanks – the more so since the American presidential lead in 2006 to cut US gasoline consumption by 20 per cent, the amount imported from the unstable Middle East. In 2004 a clutch of ministers opened the first public hydrogen filling station in the German capital. 'We are pointing the way forward for sustainable mobility,' declared Dr Manfred Stolpe, Minister of Transport, a clear indication of political will which should accelerate a new generation of fuel stops.

HYDROGEN FUEL STATION
Design for BMW
2004

AWAY–
DESIGN DESTINATIONS

ULTIMATELY,
THE CHALLENGE FACED
BY TRANSPORTATION OF
ALL KINDS IS THAT WE,
AND OUR GOODS,
NEED TO TRAVEL LESS.
HOWEVER, CHANGING
SOCIAL AND ECONOMIC
BEHAVIOUR WILL
BE A SLOW PROCESS.

TRANSPORT
IS PART OF AND
ESSENTIAL
TO THE INFRA-
STRUCTURE OF
A COUNTRY;
ITS QUALITY
SHOULD NOT BE
JUST DOWN TO
ECONOMICS

RODNEY KINSMAN

Ultimately, the challenge faced by transportation of all kinds is that we, and our goods, need to travel less. When we do travel, we need to do so responsibly. However, changing social and economic behaviours will be a slow process, as a recent report indicates.

The RAC Foundation Report into the future of transport found that today people travel three times as much as they did fifty years ago, 85 per cent of them by car, and road capacity has not kept up.[29] The next twenty-five years will see a 50 per cent increase in car travel, greater demand for rail and increased congestion. Roads generate half of Britain's pollutants, which could be modified if not eliminated, while traffic noise is a growing menace.

The report suggested that cars would provide 'living room comfort' with multimedia technology, and hybrid systems leading to fuel-cell power, by 2050, plus some degree of auto-pilotage. Trucks will remain the main means of shifting goods, using efficiencies already developed and telematics, and will be quieter, safer and more fuel-efficient. More night-time operation is likely.

The report found that the car is here to stay and bus travel will remain constant, but coaches could increase if roads are improved, while walking and cycling, having declined parri passu to car growth, could well regenerate if safety improved, but rail investment in Britain lags behind the Continent. Road pricing is a means to reducing congestion, and drivers would accept it if it meant more money spent on roads. As Kinsman points out, 'Transport is part of and essential to the infrastructure of a country; its quality should not be just down to economics.'

CONCEPT CAR
Design: Zaha Hadid
Commission: Kenny Schachter
© Zaha Hadid Architects/Kenny Schachter
2006

SIGNS FOR TOMORROW

Growing awareness of environmental pollution signals accelerating development in alternative fuels. British government scientist Sir David King recognized that 'The problem of climate change means we must look to carbon-free technologies to meet our energy needs.' Congestion is a major challenge, with one report claiming the cost to the US alone of $68 billion, 62 per cent of the cost generated in cities.

Design is therefore no longer just about style, but also about balancing market need, a mix of system, material and mode, individual aspiration and societal sensibilities. As Seymour Powell's Nick Talbot states, 'we are a selfish society; in the past people invested in the common good to help make a better future' and 'we need to accelerate the rate at which we solve problems, the sooner the better'.

The car is still king, but despite Margaret Thatcher's famous comment that 'anyone travelling on a bus over the age of thirty is a failure', public transport is not the poor man's option. There is a conflict between the individual desire for car comfort and convenience and society's need for sustainable cost-effective solutions. Mass transit has to respond within a framework of reasonable regulation.

Designer and founder of OMK Design Rodney Kinsman sensibly claims that 'one should not distinguish between modes of transport. For mass transportation people expect the same standards. Now travel is travel. It's constant.'

POWER FOR CHANGE

In the future, driving will give way to moving, commuting to working on the move, long-distance travel to moving environments – and these changes will be upon us faster than we think, within decades.

The balance of production is shifting to Asia, and the world at large is aware of the cost of energy and the finite resource of materials and fossil fuels. Overarching these socio-economic realities, digital and satellite technology have pierced the information veil, so that the West and developing world populations are joined as never before. There is an inexorable quest for alternative energy, for eco-friendly travel, for ease of access and, above all, for fair shares in resources. Use of materials must become more responsible, in some nations more than others.

THE TRANSPORT CHALLENGE OF THE NEXT FIFTY YEARS WILL BE TO USE TECHNOLOGY TO DELIVER INFRASTRUCTURE THAT WILL STIMULATE ECONOMIC GROWTH, SUPPORT SOCIAL COHESION AND BE ENVIRONMENTALLY SUSTAINABLE.

CLIVE BIRCH

It will take less time for Chinese society to move out of rural isolation than it has taken any European country. Movement of goods and people will accelerate exponentially in India as in China and, as their peoples seek material parity, the western world looks set to move away from general to particular solutions, reflecting the quest for local identity.

The rapid global appetite for fuel continues to put political and financial pressure on many nations, and as Asia continues to develop the issue is likely to become more acute. Currently, 'In fact China, with a fifth of the world's population, consumes only 4 per cent of the world's daily oil output. It imports about three million barrels a day.'[30]

Western society will learn to live with expensive energy and to optimize it for vehicle power. Individual mobility will become a global norm and developing nations will have greater influence upon design, seeking simplicity of solution just as western manufacturers may well change from mass production towards more personalized options for the car consumer.

'We have to find new routes to individual mobility,' says Clive Birch of London's Carmen's Company – the world's oldest transport body. 'The car may be king, but it is not a city beast' and 'the focus is on the journey – how to travel swiftly, safely, certainly from dedicated departure to destination in private space, but public place'. Infrastructure itself will change slowly, because of the scale of investment, but we will continue to see more landmark transportation environments.

Public transport will continue to struggle with ageing infrastructure in historic cities, while offering more comfort and better communication. Security issues and more demanding clients, suggesting a range of facilities, less price sensitive than consumer sensitive, will offset the trend towards cheaper long-haul travel. Communication will continue to explode exponentially, facilitating the monitoring and control of travel, but also enhancing the journey, through the information interface, simplified planning and purchase, and increased entertainment.

As we have seen with the now apparently ridiculous predictions for the future made by designers and architects of the past, it is dangerous to predict big change to transportation. But to enable designers to fulfil our dreams for future mobility, the ways in which we travel must evolve. As Sir David King, Chief Scientific Adviser to HM Government, recognizes, 'Putting a man on the moon was the greatest transport challenge of the past half-century. The transport challenge of the next fifty years will be to use technology to deliver infrastructure that will stimulate economic growth, support social cohesion and be environmentally sustainable.'[31]

In the future, we will move further and faster, but we will move responsibly, or we will not move at all.

FURTHER RESEARCH

Vehicle design is constantly reported in magazines, national newspapers including Daily Telegraph Motoring, motor manufacturers' periodicals, automotive and design media. There are numerous car magazines; some of the best for design are Car, Interior Motives and Intersection, and the on-line cardesignnews.com The most useful annual publication is the Car Design Yearbook: The Definitive Guide to New Concept and Production Cars Worldwide by Stephen Newbury and Giles Chapman, Merrell Publishers Ltd, issue 1, 2002 – currently on issue 6.

There are many online references, easily accessed by place name, manufacturer, marque, model or news medium. Specific documents and publications are listed.

WEBSITES

www.autodesignmagazine.com
www.cardesignnews.com
www.intersectionmagazine.com
www.carmagazine.co.uk
www.topgear.com
www.bbc.co.uk for news stories

PUBLICATIONS

Bayley, Stephen and Chapman, Giles, Moving Objects, Eye-Q Ltd, London, 1999.

Car Bored, Royal College of Art, London, 2004.

Chapman, Giles, Car Badges: The Ultimate Guide to Automotive Logos Worldwide, Merrell Publishers Ltd, London, 2005.

Chapman, Giles, SUV: the World's Greatest Sport Utility Vehicles, Merrell Publishers Ltd, London, 2005.

Crawford, J. H., Carfree Cities, International Books.

Glancey, Jonathan, The Car, a History of the Automobile, Carlton Books, London, 2004.

Innovate, Royal College of Art, London, 2005.

Kerr, Joe and Gibson, Andrew, London from Punk to Blair, Reaktion Books, London, 2003.

Kerr, Joe and Peter Wollen (eds), Autopia: cars and culture, Reaktion Books, London, 2002.

Lee, Kyung Min, Sound – the Redundancy of Dynamism, MA thesis, RCA London, 2005.

Look Both Ways, Royal College of Art, London 2003.

Brooke Hodge and Edson Armi, C., RetroFuturism, The Car Designs of J Mays, Universe Publishing, New York, 2002.

Motoring Towards 2050, RAC Foundation, London, 2002.

Move It! Royal College of Art, London, 2005.

Newbury, Stephen, The Car Design Yearbook, Merrell Publishers Ltd, London and New York, 2003 et seq.

Pawley, Martin, Terminal Architecture, Reaktion Books, London, 1998.

Research Associates Programme, Helen Hamlyn Research Foundation, London, 2005.

Sparke, Penny, A Century of Car Design, Mitchell Beazley, London, 2002.

Wollen, Peter and Kerr, Joe, Autopia: Cars and Culture, Reaktion Books, London, 2002.

All quotations in the text, unless otherwise stated, are based on interviews with the author.

1. Ian Pearson, quoted in Dream, Summer 2005.

2. See Penny Sparke, 'Introduction', A Century of Car Design, Mitchell Beazley, 2002.

3. Gary Bradshaw, Wright Brothers History: The Tale of the Airplane, 2007, www.wam.umd.edu/~stwright/WrBr/taleplane.html

4. Helen Evenden, 'Reach Out and Touch', Modernism is Movement in Cent, The Paul Priestman Issue, 2006.

5. Euan Sey, 'Brand Hatch', Interior Motives, July/August 2006.

6. Ibid.

7. Burkhard Goeschel, Director, BMW, quoted in the national press, 2005.

8. www.maybach-manufaktur.com/index.htm

9. www.carpages.co.uk/bentley/bentley-continental-flying-spur-design-19-01-05.asp

10. J. Mays, quoted in Fast Company magazine, British Council report, 2005.

11. www.designmuseum.org/design/jaguar

12. Rick Wagoner, General Motors, quoted in Autointel, 2005.

13. Dr Manfred Stolpe, German Minister of Transport, quoted in BMW marketing material, 2005.

14. Dr Thomas Weber, quoted in DaimlerChrysler marketing material, 2005.

15. Bob Swarup and Lewis Dartnell, quoted in the 2004 BASF/Telegraph older science writer competition.

16. Stevens designed and engineered Rootes' Hillman Hunter and Sunbeam Rapier and developed the 1980s' Cipher.

17. D. Nye, quoted in Driving Ambition, 1999.

18. Giles Chapman, SUV: the World's Greatest Sport Utility Vehicles, 2005.

19. David Millward, transport correspondent, Telegraph, 10 October 2005.

20. UITP Sustainability Report, Ticket to the Future, Brussels, 2003.

21. Glancey, Jonathan, London Bread and Circuses, Verso, 2001.

22. www.designmuseum.org/design/london-transport and www.ltmuseum.co.uk/

23. Alan Ponsford, quoted in Owen Evans, Helen Hamlyn Foundation Research Associate Report, Royal College of Art, 2004.

24. Vern Rayburn, quoted in www.oglemodels.com

25. Don Taylor, quoted in www.oglemodels.com

26. Hamish Scott, Telegraph, January 2006.

27. Rebecca Feiner, Telegraph, July 2005.

28. Pawley, Martin, Terminal Architecture, Reaktion Books, 1998.

29. Edmund King, RAC Foundation Report, Travel 2050.

30. BBC News, 16 February 2006, www.news.bbc.co.uk

31. Sir David King, Foreword, Intelligent Infrastructure Futures, Project Overview, 2007, www.foresight.gov.uk

INDEX